Advance Praise

"Liz Prato's profound meditations on place dislocate and then relocate understandings of Hawai'i from the point of view of the non-native visitor. She asks the good questions about white fantasies and vacation destinations while also diving into the depths of complex beauty to a land literally in the process of remaking itself. This book is a love letter to the land and people of Hawai'i, with a keen awareness that some people must let their story of this place go. A secular devotional to a place that has woven its way into Liz Prato's heart. Breathtaking."

—Lidia Yuknavitch, author of *The Chronology of Water* and *The Book of Joan*

"*Volcanoes, Palm Trees, and Privilege* is not only a breezy and appealing primer on how to negotiate both Hawai'i in all its astonishing variety and the enormous advantages and nagging burdens of privilege; it's also a moving memoir about familial loss and the reconstitution of an essential version of the self. Liz Prato is beautifully smart about how disempowerment works, and how to combat it."

—Jim Shepard, author of *Book of Aron* and *The Tunnel at the End of the Light*

"A brilliant meditation on cheeseburgers in paradise, Liz Prato's fearless and tender investigation of our complex relationship with Hawai'i will blow your mind. Hula dancers, aloha shirts, surfing, and the idyllic tropical vacation will never look the same. It's a reckoning whose time is long overdue."

—Karen Karbo, author of *In Praise of Difficult Women*, and the *Kick Ass Women* series

"For fans of Sarah Vowell and Kaui Hart Hemmings, Liz Prato's essay collection is a must-read, an essential introduction to Hawai`i that explores the islands' mythos and reality. But it's also enjoyable for those who think they know the islands well, as Prato's lyricism and playful forms offer a serious study of language, history, tourism and place. In *Volcanoes, Palm Trees, and Privilege* we witness a deeply personal tale of love, loss, and honest accounting as the author comes to understand her relationship with the islands through the crucible of family."

—Kristiana Kahakauwila, author of *This Is Paradise*

"Searching, wise, intimate and illuminating, Liz Prato's *Volcanoes, Palm Trees, and Privilege* is a complicated love letter to a place and powerful reckoning of a life. I was moved and astonished by this beautiful book."

—Cheryl Strayed, author of *Wild* and *Tiny Beautiful Things*

Cover Art and Cover Design: Cole Gerst
Interior Illustrations: Silvia Maria Aureli
Book Design: Jenny Kimura

ISBN: 978-1732610309
Printed in South Korea.

Library of Congress Control Number: 2018967483
Names: Prato, Liz, author
Title: Volcanoes, Palm Trees, and Privilege: Essays on Hawai'i/by Liz Prato—1st ed.
Description: First Edition. | Overcup Press, 2019.

Subjects:
Literature and Fiction / Essays and Correspondence / Essays
Nonfiction / Political & Social Sciences / Social Sciences / Popular Culture
Biographies and Memoirs / Essays & Correspondence / Essays
Travel / United States / West/Pacific
History / United States / State and Local / West / Hawaii

Overcup Press
4207 SE Woodstock Blvd. #253
Portland, OR 97206

lizprato.com
overcupbooks.com

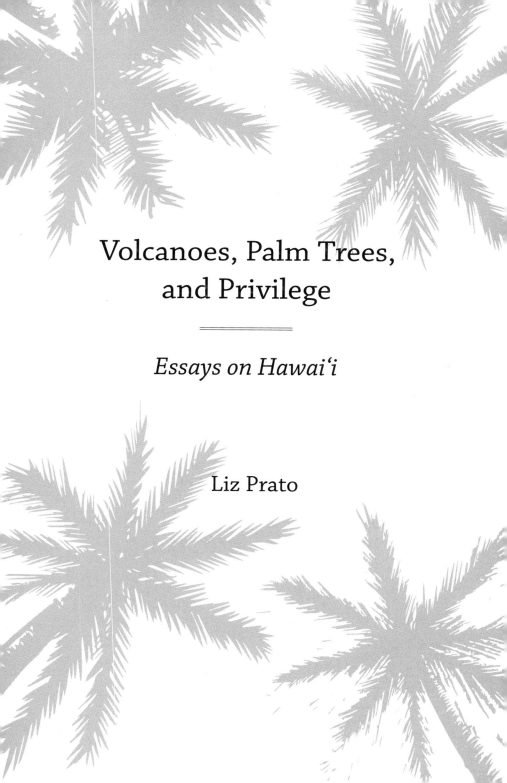

Volcanoes, Palm Trees, and Privilege

Essays on Hawai'i

Liz Prato

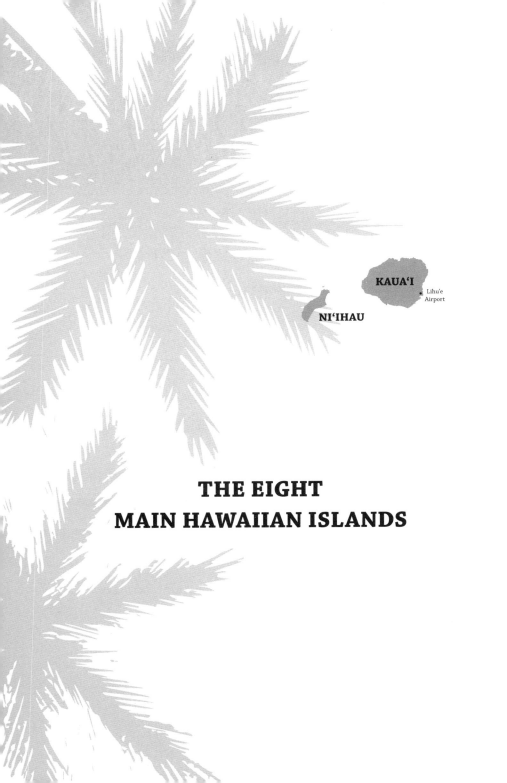

KAUAʻI

Lihuʻe
Airport

NIʻIHAU

THE EIGHT
MAIN HAWAIIAN ISLANDS

OʻAHU

Daniel K. Inouye
Airport

MOLOKAʻI

Airport

LĀNAʻI •Airport

Kahului
Airport

MAUI

KAHOʻOLAWE

Kona
Airport

Hilo
Airport

**THE
ISLAND OF HAWAIʻI
(THE BIG ISLAND)**

Contents

Dedicated to the people of Hawai'i,
past, present, and future.

A Note About the Text

THE AUTHOR HAS MADE EVERY EFFORT TO PRESERVE THE original ʻokina and kahakō in Hawaiian words, except in the case of brand names or direct quotes in which they were not previously used. For example, "Kahalā" has a kahakō over the last letter, but "Kahala Hilton" does not; when the author uses the word "Hawaiʻi," she includes the okina between the two i's, but writes "Hawaii" where Joan Didion did not.

To 'Okina, or Not to 'Okina

The most fascinating detail I learned on my first trip to Hawai'i when I was twelve years old is that the Hawaiian alphabet consists of only thirteen letters. For many years I considered this a profound metaphor about Native Hawaiians' organic wisdom and simplicity: while white Americans needed twenty-six letters to prattle on about our lives, Hawaiians managed to say everything they needed to say in only thirteen. To express love, war, land, water, hunger, birth, thirst, fire, family, death—all they required was a, e, i, o, u, h, k, l, m, n, p, w, and the mysterious 'okina.

It wasn't until well into adulthood—after over a dozen trips to the Islands—that I realized these thirteen letters were not endemic to the Hawaiians. These letters exist because white Americans assigned them to represent Native Hawaiians' oral communication. Prior to Western contact, the sole written language of the Hawaiians had been petroglyphs: simple but evocative drawings of waves and warriors, volcanoes and rain, turtles and sharks carved into rock. This can be seen as a primitive form of communication, or as evidence that story is art, and art is story.

When British explorer James Cook and his men first landed on Kaua'i in 1778, they made an initial stab at transcribing 'ōlelo Hawai'i (the Hawaiian language) into the written word. Cook and his crew seemed to have a genuine social and scientific interest in what and who they encountered on their world voyages, and their journals contributed greatly to Western understanding of native cultures. Ultimately, Cook's contact with Hawai'i also led to the archipelago's colonization, which includes capitalism (and its kissing cousin, tourism), Christianity, ecological destruction, and a handful of deadly diseases. But on his inaugural trip to the Islands, Cook sailed away with sketches of natives surfing, notes about birds and plants, and 229 Hawaiian words phonetically transcribed in his journals.

Forty years after Cook's first contact, white New England missionaries came to Hawai'i with the express goal of translating the way the Hawaiians spoke into a written language, into *their* written language. The natives and their homeland were considered dark, savage, heathen. The missionaries vowed to teach them the Bible and, you know, make them Christians. These missionaries weren't playing, either: they brought an entire wood and iron Ramage printing press on their five-month voyage down the eastern coast of North and South America, through the Strait of Magellan, and out toward Hawai'i.

The missionaries who translated Native Hawaiians' spoken language through the prism of their familiar alphabet originally included the letters b, d, r, t, and v, along with the thirteen letters that are currently recognized (Cook's linguist did the same). But the missionaries ended up dropping those five letters four years later because they were considered phonetically redundant, or the usage of them wasn't consistent among the different islands. In 1826 they actually voted on which letters to keep and which to jettison, as if it was an episode of *The Voice*. Like, "I find the b to be kind of one-dimensional," or "I'm just not *feeling* the t."

One linguistic move the missionaries made that shows respect for the Hawaiian tongue is inserting the ʻokina into words. An ʻokina looks like this: ʻ. Like a backwards, upside-down apostrophe. Many English word-processing programs don't have an ʻokina built into their software, so apostrophes are used in their place—when they aren't omitted altogether. But make no mistake: these apostrophes are imposters. They are not the real deal.

The ʻokina represents what linguists call a glottal stop, which is basically a quick, sharp pause. In ʻōlelo Hawaiʻi, the ʻokina is most often used between double vowels, indicating that you pronounce them both, like in "Hawaiʻi." But it can also appear at the front of a word that begins with a vowel, creating a short intake of breath before speaking. It's subtler than I'm making it sound, and has the effect of making words richer, more textured, like a musical note moving up and down the operatic scale. Contrary to popular (Western) belief, the ʻokina is not simply a punctuation mark. The missionaries designated the ʻokina as the thirteenth *letter* of the Hawaiian alphabet—an actual consonant in and of itself.

Hawaiian words can have drastically different meanings depending on whether or not that ʻokina is there. ʻAhi, for instance, is "tuna," while ahi is "fire." Kaʻi means "to walk," and kai means "ocean." Kou is a kind of tree, while ko'u means "my." English speakers are quite used to homographs and apparently find no reason to provide intrinsic clues to differentiate between *this one* or *that one* (does "just" mean "only," or does it mean "fair"? Is something an object, or do you object to it? Do you wave to say hello to someone, or is that a wave crashing in towards the shore?), but I bet foreign speakers wish for a little more definition inherent in our words.

When you read enough literature about Hawai'i, you notice vast inconsistencies around use of the 'okina. Many publications omit it, including an astounding number of travel guides—even ones created by Hawaiian tourism boards. From what I can tell, the roots of the anti-'okina issue go back to 1898, when the United States annexed Hawai'i and declared English its official language. It meant 'ōlelo Hawai'i was no longer taught in schools, and all governmental documents relating to Hawai'i were written in American English. Therefore, when Hawai'i became a state in 1959, and a state seal and a state constitution were created, the 'okina—and 'ōlelo Hawai'i—was nowhere to be seen. This seems especially dickish, since it was US missionaries who created and taught 'ōlelo Hawai'i, making the Islands one of the most literate societies on Earth. Then the US government quickly turned around and took that away in a linguistic bait and switch that—*hey, what do you know!*—disempowered Hawaiians.

An ever-evolving movement for restoring Native Hawaiian culture that started pretty much the *second* Westerners landed in Hawai'i got 'ōlelo Hawai'i named an official co-language of the state in 1978. And yet many authors and publications still exclude the 'okina, or use it inconsistently. The reason these publications don't use the marks—when they give an explanation at all—is that it would be too confusing or too difficult to suddenly start using them. This strikes me as *so weird*. English speakers have somehow managed to incorporate all sorts of foreign marks—accents and umlauts and tildes (the latter, by the way, is technically also a letter, and not just an n with a wavy thing over it)—without our minds being blown and, more importantly, while showing respect for the cultural origins of these words. Can you imagine the hissy fit Americans would throw if another culture decided to eliminate the c, or the k, or the q from our language because they seem redundant and it would just be *easier*? Then again, the US government has yet to be conquered. That seems to be key in dictating language: who's in charge.

I have made the decision to use the 'okina in my writing out of respect for Hawaiian culture. During the last four decades I have visited the Islands over two dozen times, and the fact that I don't remember exactly how many trips I've taken is an embarrassment of privilege. Over the years my family and I have stayed in a minimum of forty-five shoreline hotel rooms and a dozen condos, the construction of which destroyed the natural habitats of Hawaiian monk seals, albatross, and green sea turtles, and took over beaches that used to belong to the locals—if not in title, then in heart. In those hotel rooms and condos, we've taken long, hot showers, and turned on the air conditioning instead of opening windows to the trade winds.

We've left the lights on when we exited the room—not always out of forgetfulness, but because we wanted the room to seem welcoming when we returned at night. The fact that electricity is almost three times more expensive in Hawai'i than the national average was someone else's problem. The hotels and condos we stayed in were in lushly planted resorts often built on red, dry desert, and we've swam in elaborate pools requiring hundreds of thousands of gallons of water, never realizing (or caring) that being surrounded by an ocean is not at all the same as having abundant drinking water. We've flown over one hundred and seventy-five thousand miles, almost three-quarters of the distance to the moon, burning around seventeen tons of fuel. We've driven a minimum of thirty-five rental cars, spewing carbon dioxide into the air. We have laughed at the words "Mele Kalikimaka." We have benefited from our government taking land away from the Hawaiians and building on it and even bombing the shit out of it. We, white mainland Americans, have taken enough from Hawai'i. The very least I can do is not strip the 'okina away, too.

Da Kine

Da kine is a ubiquitous Hawaiian Pidgin term that lacks a specific definition because it can mean nearly anything. It's often used when the speaker can't think of or doesn't know the right word, like saying "whatchamacallit" or "thingimajig" or "you know what I mean, yeah?" It can refer to a person, place, or thing. It's generally good, and sometimes means *really* good. Context is important. Like, if someone says, "The waves are da kine!" they most likely mean, "The waves are awesome!" not, "The waves were whatchamacallit." If someone says, "You bring da kine?" they probably mean, "Did you bring the stuff?" That feels like the most accurate definition of da kine: stuff. Where is the stuff? How is stuff? That is the *stuff*, man! It occurs to me this all sounds very much like the vocabulary employed by drug culture—a largely coincidental and convenient bonus of da kine.

The forthcoming "Da Kine" sections are a combination of whatchamacallits and awesomes! These quick grinds (that's Pidgin for "yummy bites") are familiar and essential aspects of the diverse and textured quilt that is Hawaiian culture.

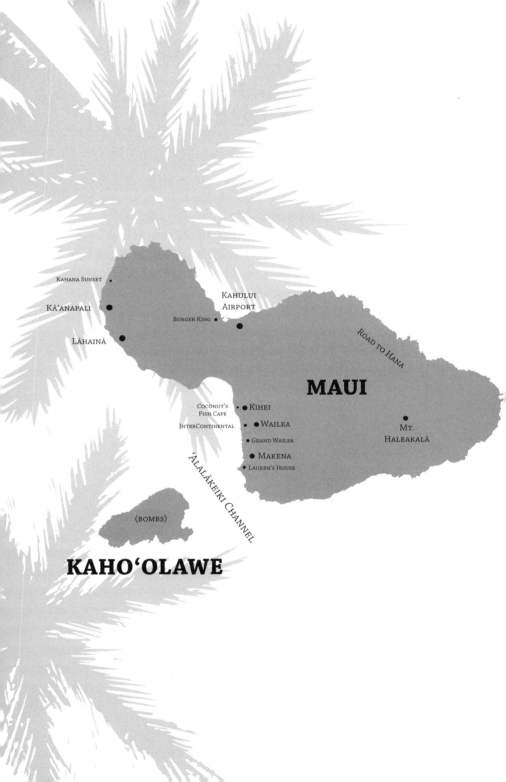

KAHANA SUNSET

KAHULUI
AIRPORT

KĀʻANAPALI

BURGER KING

LĀHAINĀ

ROAD TO HANA

MAUI

COCONUT'S
FISH CAFE

KIHEI

WAILEA

INTERCONTINENTAL

GRAND WAILEA

MT.
HALEAKALĀ

MAKENA

LAUREN'S HOUSE

ʻALALĀKEIKI CHANNEL

(BOMBS)

KAHOʻOLAWE

Flying Under Assumed Names

MY FAMILY WAS STUCK INSIDE A WHITE RENTAL CAR during a crazy-ass rainstorm on our first trip to Maui. We'd gotten a flat tire somewhere between our condo north of Kaʻanapali and the former whaling village of Lāhainā. This was not a mainland highway like I-25 back in Denver—four lanes of asphalt speeding each way—but a rural Maui highway. All around us, five-foot sugarcane stalks bent and blew in the wind, while the sky dumped rain in that way you usually only see in movies. It was March of 1979, and I was twelve and my brother, Steve, was fourteen. With his birthday in December and mine in June, there were always six months where it appeared he was two years older than me, and six months where it seemed we were only a year apart. Together, apart, close, and then not.

We were waiting to be rescued by someone from the rental car company. I'm not sure why my dad couldn't just change the tire. First, my memory tells me it's because we had two flat tires, and there was only one spare in the truck. And then my brain insists that we had only one flat, but the rental car company neglected to stock the car with a single spare. My mind comes up with these different explanations because it can't imagine how my dad, who labored in the southern Colorado mines as a teenager and served on an aircraft carrier during World War II, could not be bothered to change a tire in the rain for his wife and kids.

From the vantage of the twenty-first century, it's hard to imagine how, exactly, we thought or knew someone from the rental car company would come rescue us. We had no cell phones; it was still five years until ye old "brick" was available to consumers for around $4,000 and weighing in at two pounds. No pay phones dotted the rural highway. I think what happened is another driver—a local or a tourist—stopped to ask if we needed help, and told us that they'd call the rental car company when they got into Lāhainā. We trusted them to do so, and I will have to trust my memory, because there is no one to ask, no one else in that car still alive, to fill in my gaps.

* * *

Both my parents were raised in poverty, and the middle-class comforts I'd taken for granted my whole life—a four-bedroom house, a sprawling manicured lawn, two new cars in the garage—were novel to them. We usually took two trips a year: spring break in San Diego and a summer road trip to Big Springs, Nebraska. In San Diego we stayed at Vacation Village, a fantasy concept resort (although the specific fantasy remains unclear) with beach bungalows, a Gaudí-esque spired tower, and a bar that could double as a bomb shelter (hello, Cold War!). We built sandcastles and tootled around Mission Bay on a motorboat and got splashed by Shamu at SeaWorld. In the summer on my aunt and uncle's farm in Big Springs, I helped my cousins feed the pigs and milk the cows and gather eggs, while Steve rode around on tractors and combines.

Our first trip to Hawai'i signified that my dad's socioeconomic status had changed. We flew first class on United Airlines on one of those completely awesome/now obsolete 747s with a spiral staircase leading to a groovy upstairs lounge, where my family played five-card draw for pennies. The stewardesses wore floral dresses and handed us actual printed menus. The cover sported a drawing of a Hawaiian chief—maybe King Kamehameha—holding up a friendly hand as if to say, "Howdy, white folks!" The meal choices weren't exotic (or particularly Hawaiian for that matter): prime rib or teriyaki chicken, with coffee, tea, or Sanka, but it was surely a step above whatever miscellaneous meat and mushy rice concoction was going on back in coach. I recently bought one of the menus off eBay for $35, which is arguably a ridiculous amount for kitschy nostalgia, but maybe a reasonable price to pay for memory.

I'd never known anyone who'd been to Hawai'i. My only ideas of it were gleaned from *The Brady Bunch* episodes where Bobby stole a native tiki idol and the family got a shit-ton of bad luck. The combination of my excitement, an early morning departure, and the longest plane ride I'd ever been on blurred my memory of what it was like to first step foot on Hawaiian ground. I don't even remember if we got a lei greeting like the Brady clan did when they descended the open-air staircase onto the Honolulu Airport tarmac. But the one enduring sensory detail is that the air smelled like flowers. The humid trade winds blowing through my curly hair were sweet and spicy and slightly hot pink.

We started our Adventure in Paradise!™ at the Kahala Hilton, one of the two hotels Joan Didion visited during her frequent jaunts to Hawai'i—not that I knew who Joan Didion was back then. Most of her island essays recount her time at Waikīkī's Royal Hawaiian hotel, a symbol of inclusion in a privileged class that she never apologized for being a part of. The Royal Hawaiian (aka: the Royal, the Pink Palace, and the Pink Lady) is where Didion escaped to in 1969 to recover from feeling disconnected from modern society and its disintegrating morals. I don't know if she was aware of the irony of fleeing to one of the most isolated archipelagos in the world to cure her sense of isolation. But that's not the only reason Didion was in Honolulu in 1969 with her husband and young daughter: they were in Hawai'i to try to circumvent a divorce. Maybe that was a thing married couples did, even ten years later. Maybe a more discreet campaign of the Hawai'i Tourism Authority is "A Last-Ditch Attempt to Save One's Marriage." Maybe that's why my family was taking this exotic, expensive vacation, despite my parents sleeping in separate bedrooms for the past six months.

Even though my dad was keen on experiencing—and treating his family to—the luxuries he never knew as a child, he never, not once, wanted to stay at the Royal Hawaiian. I wonder if it's because the hotel was converted into R&R headquarters for US military men during World War II, with barbed wire separating it from the beach. Although the Pink Palace was returned to its luxury prestige after the war, it's easy to see how a veteran of the Pacific theater might forever view it as a refuge for men hoping to escape the trauma of guns and bombs and bodies.

At the Kahala Hilton, we stayed in a large lagoon-side room with two queen beds—Mom and I slept in one, and Steve and Dad in the other. In the morning we stepped onto our lānai (the Hawaiian word for patio, I learned), and in the lagoon right in front of us were dolphins swimming and splashing and arcing through the air. Steve and I built sandcastles and splashed in the pool...or at least I assume we did. The Pacific Ocean, the sunshine, the palm trees, the sand, all blurred together into one Technicolor scene: family vacation at the beach.

We joined the masses at Pearl Harbor to visit the USS *Arizona* Memorial. Whenever I read about the Pearl Harbor tour now, it describes tourists being ferried to the memorial on small harbor boats, passing battleships both in and out of service. I don't remember that *at all*. I remember standing in a line, and I remember it was really hot, and I'm pretty sure I was really bored. My interest in war-related stuff only extended as far as some way to connect with my dad. I do remember standing on the whisper-quiet monument, looking over the railing. It didn't make sense to me, what we were seeing, what was lost, until I bought a postcard of an aerial view. Underneath where we'd stood was the dark outline of the battleship, as if it and the 1,177 men trapped on board had sunk straight down without a fight.

This is what it means for an event to live in infamy. It is not just witnessed, but the details are painstakingly

recorded and memorialized so that long after all those wit-
nesses die, it will still live in the collective consciousness.
But what if there was no iconic radio broadcast, no giant
newspaper headlines, no austere monument constructed
to commemorate an event, to corroborate its veracity, to
honor the dead? What if there is no one to ask, no one
still alive to fill in the gaps? Then we turn to the unreliable
partnership between neural circuitry and faith to cement
this thing called memory.

* * *

After a few days in Honolulu, my family took the forty-five minute flight to Maui, where we stayed in the
Kahana Sunset condominiums. Decades later I learned
the word kahana means "turning point" in Hawaiian, but I
still contend back then I didn't know my family was about
to enter the one-way curve of a hairpin turn. Each brown
unit at the Kahana Sunset had an AstroTurfed lānai where
my dad and I took pictures of each other holding my
hand-drawn signs that said, "Hey, I'm in Hawaii!" and
"Look whose [sic] in Hawaii!" Mom and I slept on twin
beds in the dimly lit second bedroom, and Dad and Steve
shared the sunny master. Sharing a room with my mom
was fun, like an extended slumber party. I could swear I
remember us sitting on the bed brushing each other's hair,
although I also admit to possibly fabricating this idealized
memory to represent how much I loved my mom.

Since none of us seemed to be questioning why we
were all taking this exotic vacation together, the island of
Maui wanted to make it perfectly clear: you all, together,

is a *bad* idea. A few highlights of our Adventure in Paradise!™ included: Our car got a flat tire in the middle of a tropical rainstorm. On a whale-watching tour we only saw the very tip-top of one or two humpbacks far away, and I could have been easily convinced they were just logs or other jetsam. The Kahana Sunset hosted a mahi-mahi barbeque that resulted in a widespread case of food poisoning, taking down my dad with diarrhea for two days—Kamehameha's revenge, Steve and I called it. Then, at midnight on March 31, when we were packed and ready to return to Denver, the United Airlines mechanists union went on strike, leaving us with no way to get home.

The mechanists wanted the pay of their top-rate mechanics raised from $10.00 per hour to $13.14 per hour over the next three years. It's kind of hard to understand how $13.00 per hour is unreasonable, considering these folks make sure your plane is in proper working order before it lofts thirty-five thousand feet into the air. A handy-dandy inflation calculator tells me that in 1979, $13.00 was roughly equivalent to $46.00 in today's money, which does seem like a lot. Minimum wage was $2.90, and gas cost $0.86 a gallon. But between 1978 and 1979, inflation had risen from 7.6 percent to 11.2 percent—a mind-blowing 47 percent. The 1970s' skyrocketing food prices, unusually high mortgage rates, and a second oil crisis (thanks a *lot*, Iran) had the general public freaked about how to keep pace with the cost of living. And while the average American worker might not have had any bargaining power to address their panic, the eighteen thousand United Airlines employees who belonged to the International Association of Machinists and Aerospace Workers did. When United declared their proposed raise too much, the mechanists struck.

Fun fact: an airline can't function without mechanists, and they aren't easily replaced by scabs. United Airlines was crippled and forced to shut down, stranding the one hundred and thirty thousand passengers on their daily flight manifest.

It never occurred to my parents to extend our stay in Hawai'i for even one extra day to sort out how we'd get home, and Steve and I didn't petition for that option, either. I mean, I actually wanted to go back to *school.* We just headed straight for the Maui airport to figure it out on the fly (no pun intended). It was easy enough to get to Honolulu via an interisland airline, where sign-carrying strikers marched on the sidewalk. Years later, after I cleaned out both my parents' houses, I found an old homework assignment I'd completed sometime after the trip that looked like this:

Think of a specific event where something happened
- TIME: *Last spring on my Hawaii trip*
- PLACE: *Airport; airplane*
- PEOPLE: *My mom, my dad, my brother and me*
- WHAT HAPPENED: *Flight was canceled and our airline went on strike*
- HOW YOU FELT: *Angry at the airline and like throwing rocks at the people striking*

I don't actually remember being angry and wanting to throw rocks at the strikers. I wonder if I was, but decades of time and space have dissipated the fury and only left me with images, voices, moist heat, the spicy-sweet smell of flowers. But in my experience, that's not how anger and memory work. The rush of adrenaline, the tensing of muscles, the quickening of heart and breath grabs onto neural pathways with more tenacity than the delicacy of scenery and sound. There's not a date on the homework assignment, but under "Time" I wrote, "Last spring," which means the assignment was from fall of 1979 or winter of the following year, which means I completed it either right before or right after my parents told us they were getting divorced. And maybe that's why I wanted to throw rocks.

* * *

I wandered around the airport gift shop to kill time (I still do this every time I fly) wearing a lime green muumuu and plastic magenta lei, while Dad schemed to get us out of Hawai'i. The gift shop cashier complimented me on my lei—the quintessential symbol of tacky touristic appropriation—and suggested I rub its plastic petals with plumeria perfume so they'd smell like real flowers. When Dad finally sat down next to me for a break, I said, "The cashier in the gift shop gave me a tip." I held up my lei and the little bottle of perfume I'd bought, and smiled.

Dad looked tired and confused. "A tip? What do you mean?"

I rolled my eyes to indicate how *incredibly stupid* he was for not knowing exactly what my vague gestures and props meant.

Dad finally finagled us some other passengers' tickets to LAX, but they couldn't be transferred into our names. We had to fly under assumed names: the Pratos became the Yamamuras, and I was Phyllis. Still technically the same family, but not the same. In my family's waning moments as an intact foursome, we weren't even the Pratos anymore.

We flew coach on a Western Airlines plane that appeared to be dragged out of mothballs (that's what my mom said at the time, so it's what I've been saying for thirty-nine years). My seat wouldn't go into its full and upright position, so a frazzled flight attendant (our big joke was that the flight attendants were pulled out of mothballs, too!) attempted to fix it with a bottle opener. The bottle opener proved to be a worthless mechanical tool, so I just laid back for the flight to Los Angeles, reading Judy Blume and *Tiger Beat* magazine and eating my coach lunch, which really wasn't all that bad.

At LAX we crossed more picket lines, and Dad ran from ticket counter to ticket counter trying to get us home. He decided we should fly to Las Vegas. People in Vegas, he reasoned, often missed flights because they were drunk or had to cash in their plane ticket to pay gambling debt or simply lost track of the hour in the dusky, timeless casinos. When the four of us landed at McCarran it was almost 9:00 p.m., our luggage was god knows where, we had stopped speaking to each other somewhere between

LAX and the desert and were miserably gliding down the moving walkway. We slid past a Continental Airlines gate with a flight leaving for Salt Lake City in five minutes. "Do you have any seats?" Dad called to the ticket agent.

"We have two!" she called back. We ran to the end of the walkway, and Mom and I were ushered onto the flight to Salt Lake City—that much closer to Denver. That much farther away from my dad and Steve.

Everything was closed when the taxi took us to the Marriott in Salt Lake City. We couldn't even find a place to buy a toothbrush. "Wow, they really roll up the carpets early here," Mom said—even though it was 11:00 p.m. This was no longer a fun slumber party with Mom, but through no fault of her own: she never complained, snapped, yelled, or made me feel otherwise terrible. It was as if we were aware that very soon this would make a funny story. We slept in a king bed, woke up very early the next morning, went back to the airport, and found another plane home. Home. Home.

Our luggage arrived at our front door the next day, and Mom did laundry and I went to school. We ate what we wanted to eat for dinner without having to consider the needs and desires of my brother or dad. They stayed in Vegas for another three days—they were "stuck" there, they claimed, at the MGM Grand. Mom and I both knew no one got stuck in Vegas. They needed a vacation from our vacation, and we weren't exactly complaining. Those three days were like a test run of how our lives would be less than a year later: Mom and I making our own decisions, Steve and Dad making theirs, the four of us no longer a family in the traditional sense. Two houses with two drastically different incomes. I was able to swim between the two economies, living with my mom where we'd save up to eat out and buy clothes, and vacationing with my dad in hotels with room service and turquoise pools.

Dad and Steve's extended layover in Vegas inspired Dad to take us back to the MGM that summer, and the next summer, too. Three months after our last trip, the MGM caught fire and eighty-seven people died. Steve and Dad and I never went to Vegas together again, but I can't tell you if that had anything to do with the fire—if it was causational, correlational, or coincidence. I just know that's when my dad decided to give Hawaiʻi another shot. We went to Waikīkī (where we stayed at the Sheraton, *not* the Royal Hawaiian), and two years after our failed first trip, my dad, brother, and I returned to Maui—without my mom. It was the beginning of my lifelong love affair with Hawaiʻi, one that would always be mixed with loss. I didn't know until recently how loss, itself, is so thoroughly the story of Hawaiʻi, and how I would be immersed in that story for decades to come.

Da Kine | The Kahakō

THE KAHAKŌ IS ANOTHER MARK THAT IS SOMETIMES used—and sometimes abandoned—in written Hawaiian. The kahakō is the dash above a vowel indicating you pronounce the long sound of the vowel, like nēnē or kāne (the Hawaiian words for "goose" and "man," respectively). The kahakō doesn't inspire quite as much impassioned debate as the 'okina, but it's still in the mix. I read an Editor's Note in *Hawaiian Business Magazine* that discussed their year-after-year debate about whether or not to use the "diacritical marks" 'okina and kahakō in their publication. This confused me, because I'm under the distinct impression that the 'okina is not "just" a diacritical mark, but is a consonant in the Hawaiian alphabet. The kahakō isn't a consonant (it's a macron!), which doesn't mean it's not important, but certainly makes it more confusing as to whether or not I should use it. [Note: The magazine has since reversed their stance—sort of. They're trying to incorporate the 'okina and the kahakō in limited ways, and—get this—the original issue containing the Editor's Note has mysteriously disappeared from the internet.] But just as I wouldn't leave off the accent grave if I was writing about French culture, I won't leave off the kahakō when writing about Hawaiian. For one simple reason: it's kind of assholish.

A Haole Guide to Hawaiian Taxonomy

MOST TOURIST GUIDEBOOKS ARE QUICK TO REMIND readers that Hawai'i is part of the United States, and therefore referring to the mainland as "the States" is a major breach of etiquette, fairly insulting, and also kind of stupid. After all, much is made of Hawai'i being our fiftieth state. Hawai'i is responsible for giving symmetry to the rows of stars on the US flag. President Barack Obama is from Hawai'i and, as much as some people wanted to pretend he's not an American, Hawai'i is not a foreign country. Hawaiians are Americans.

Here's where it gets tricky: You know how people who live in Vermont are called Vermonters, and people from Colorado are Coloradans, and folks from Oregon are Oregonians? In the Islands, someone who lives in Hawai'i is not called a Hawaiian, but a "resident of Hawai'i." Only direct descendants of Native Hawaiians are called Hawaiian. They can also be called kanaka maoli. A permanent or longtime resident of Hawai'i is kama'āina, and newcomers are malihini. If someone is born in Hawai'i but is *not* white (if they are of Japanese, Chinese, Filipino, Korean, etc. descent), then they are called a local. A white person is called a haole, which once meant "foreigner," and some people believe translates as "without breath." White people, regardless of how long they've lived in Hawai'i, are never called local, but they can be kama'āina. It's like a logic problem you'd find in a grocery store puzzle magazine: if locals can be kama'āina, and haoles can be kama'āina, but haoles can never be locals, then....

There's a pretty big difference between the definition of "Hawaiian" as used by the United States Census, and as used in Hawai'i for legal or identity purposes. The census used to include "Pacific Islanders" in the Asian category, but Native Hawaiian activists convinced them to create a separate category for Native Hawaiian and Other Pacific Islanders (NHPI). Frankly, that doesn't clear things up all that much, since not all Pacific Islanders are Native Hawaiian, but *all* Native Hawaiians are Pacific Islanders (the logic problem rears its ugly head again).

Native Hawaiians—the people who settled the archipelago somewhere between 300 and 800 CE—originally hailed from the Marquesas Islands. The next group to arrive was from Tahiti. Pacific Islanders *do* include Tahitians and Marquesans, and also encompass people from Samoa, Fiji, Tonga, the Gambier Islands, the Cook Islands, the Mariana Islands, Melanesia, Micronesia...

Et cetera.

To even further complicate matters, it's hypothesized that Tahiti (whose voyagers conquered the Marquesans when they arrived in Hawai'i) was itself first settled by the Marquesans, and the Marquesas Islands were settled by Samoans, who came from Southeast Asia and Melanesia. We can keep following this line of human migration all the way back to Africa, as trips through human migration tend to go, but because I'm trying to understand what it means to be Native Hawaiian and/ or Pacific Islander, that's exactly where I'm going to stop. In the Hawaiian Islands.

The particular designation of NHPI matters mainly for the purpose of the census, which is about counting and—ironically—not about the law. This naming matters in a whole different way legally. In 1921, a bill called The Hawaiian Homes Commission Act passed in the US Congress with the intent of giving land back to the Hawaiian people. By this time, it was pretty well recognized that the US presence in the archipelago had demolished the Hawaiian culture (not to mention the population, through the introduction of whooping cough, small pox, and venereal diseases), so Congress figured returning some of their land might help make things right. Hawaiian Home Lands, as they're officially called, can range in size from a quarter-acre lot that may or may not have a house on it, to multi-acre agricultural lands. They are leased to Native Hawaiians for only $1 per year for 99 years with limited property taxes.

While this sounds like a good way to begin making reparations to Native Hawaiians, there is so much incredibly fucked up about this program that it's hard to know where to begin. Although, in a sense, you don't have to look further than 1921, since the most controversial aspect of the law has never once been amended. In the rest of the United States, who "counts" as a Native American and partakes in tribal membership is set individually by each tribe and varies from as low as one-sixteenth blood quantum up to one-half. Prince Kūhiō Kalanianaʻole, Hawaiʻi's congressional delegate in 1920 (one without a vote), lobbied that Hawaiians be no less than 1/32 blood quantum to receive Home Lands. But Congress decided not to listen to the Hawaiian guy. They decided that in order to qualify for Home Lands, people must prove 50 percent blood relation to residents of Hawaiʻi before Western contact in 1778. Many scholars theorize that this number was set so high because Congress assumed not many people would have that high a percentage of Native Hawaiian blood (or be able to prove they did), or that they would die/be bred out, and then the government wouldn't have to cough up a lot of land.

Not only is that scenario not the case—there's a really long waiting list to get Hawaiian Home Lands—but it also screws people of authentic Native Hawaiian background who fall short of the 50 percent minimum. And in case that's not ridiculous enough: currently, DNA or any other genetic testing are not acceptable means of proving one's ancestry. It has to be proven through paperwork—birth certificates, marriage certificates, death certificates, etc. The rule assumes a certain bureaucratic record-keeping is in place, despite there being no written language in Hawaiʻi prior to the 1820s. And if you happen to be adopted and therefore aren't legally allowed to know your genealogy? Well, good luck with that.

Several news sources that you'd think would be reliable—like the *Honolulu Star-Advertiser* and *Al Jazeera*—say the waiting list for Home Lands is twenty-nine thousand people long. I went to the Department of Hawaiian Home Lands (DHHL) website and clicked on the waiting list tab, and it showed over forty-four thousand plus-change had applied. Each person was listed individually, and although I didn't count each name, a rough accounting proved forty-four thousand to be more or less accurate. Weirdly, there's another page on the same website that claims twenty-nine thousand people are waiting. The reason for the significant discrepancy is not clear, not even after I waded through reams of official documents acquired through interlibrary loan and was reminded why I didn't "do anything" with that history degree I earned in college. In the same article where the twenty-nine thousand figure is cited, *Al Jazeera* interviewed an 80-year-old man who has been on the waiting list since he was twenty—sixty frickin' years. He wants an agricultural plot on Kaua'i so he can raise cattle and grow his own food, like his family did when he was a child. This guy wants to maintain a distinctly Hawaiian way of living from the 'āina, which is expressly stated as a primary goal of the Hawaiian Homes Commission Act. The reason he's never received land isn't because there's none available. There are designated and deserted Home Lands not far from where he lives. The government won't give him a parcel of this conveniently located land because it lacks services, like a water and sewer line and a road. This guy's like, "Hey, just because there's not municipal water doesn't mean there's not water" (when someone is used to living on the land—a tropical, fairly rainy one, at that—they can figure out how to get water, you know?), and he's willing to build a road. But no. This man will most likely perish on the waiting list.

One of the good(?) things about dying on the waiting list is that applicants can name a successor to their place on the list—assuming, of course, the heir is 50 percent Hawaiian. They don't lose their place in line, although I'm not sure how much that matters, since applications aren't processed in the order in which they were received. Leafing through the minutes of DHHL meetings (once again reminding me of why I'm not a historian), I found the successor application for one George Keolanui, who died in 2014. He applied for a residential plot in 1969, languishing on the wait list for forty-five years.

But you know who doesn't languish on the list for forty-five years? A whole bevy of *non*-Hawaiian people and *corporations*. You see, the Hawaiian Homes Commission Act contains a gigantic loophole that allows the government to lease "unused" Home Lands to non-natives. The problem is that *why* the lands are or can be deemed unused is not clarified. Perhaps the original sponsors of the act thought that after all the land was handed out to every single eligible Hawaiian, there'd be a surplus (an optimistic and probably naïve reading of their intentions). But without that—or *any*—specificity written into the law, the interpretation is left up to the Home Lands committee. It's estimated that around *half* of all available Home Lands have been leased to non-natives. A few examples include: a non-Hawaiian couple with a five-thousand-acre ranch on Maui, a mainland developer building a 1.4-million-square-foot mall on West Oʻahu, and—wait for the gag reflex—a Target on the Big Island.

To be clear, the DHHL isn't stupid; they don't charge Target (and Safeway and Walmart) $1 per year. DeBartolo Development, the builder of the megamall on Oʻahu, will pay the DHHL $142 million during the first twenty-five years of the lease—which is handy, since the DHHL is in gigantic debt. Not only do they lease land for $1 a year to Hawaiians, they also provide them with loans to improve their property and build houses. But the DHHL isn't a bank. They ended up drowning in red ink, and stealing Home Lands from Hawaiians and leasing them out for big bucks was their way to get afloat again. Which does make them sound sort of stupid—not being able to foresee the cash flow problem—but it's a flaw of the original law more so than the contemporary handlers. Because it's a federal program, it would literally take an act of Congress to change the law, and with their level of effectiveness… well, you can see the problem. (And, let's face it: if it didn't happen when Hawaiian-born Obama was in office, it's a lost cause). On the other hand, it's nothing short of a miracle that the twenty-nine thousand or forty-four thousand people on the waiting list don't bring one mother of a class-action lawsuit against the DHHL. Maybe they aren't as litigious in Hawaiʻi as we are on the mainland.

So this incredibly screwed-up program is the main reason being 50 percent Hawaiian matters at all. It might even be the only reason, since many citizens of Hawaiʻi believe it doesn't matter if your blood is one drop Hawaiian or 100 percent. Hawaiian is Hawaiian is Hawaiian. But just to add a plot twist—and to contradict my earlier statement that Hawaiians are Americans—there's a contingent of Native Hawaiians who don't believe they are United States citizens. They don't accept that Hawai'i is a US state. Once again, we don't have to travel very far back in history to understand why. In 1893, some cranky sugar plantation owners and the US Marines staged a coup against the Hawaiian monarchy and deposed Queen Lili'uokalani. Seizing the Kingdom of Hawai'i is why the United States had the power to annex it in 1898, which is why they could make it a state in 1959. But the coup was *illegal* (as I assume most coups are), and in 1993 President Bill Clinton even issued an official statement of apology to the people of Hawai'i for the illegal overthrow of their government. That acknowledgment didn't undo Hawai'i's statehood, though, so members of the Hawaiian Sovereignty Movement continue to declare that they are not Americans, but citizens of the Kingdom of Hawai'i, which has been under constant military occupation since 1893. I assume this means they don't fill out the census.

Those who do fill out the census and identify themselves as "Native Hawaiian or other Pacific Islander" only officially comprise 9.9 percent of Hawai'i's population. If 90 percent of the residents of Hawai'i aren't Hawaiian, then what are they? Thirty-seven percent identify as Asian alone (Japanese, Chinese, Filipino, Korean, Vietnamese, Thai, etc.), 26.7 percent white alone (aka: haole), and 2.6 percent black alone, which leaves us with about 23 percent of the population that is of two or more races. These folks may or may not be called hapa, depending on who you ask.

My haole friend Edie was born and raised in Hawai'i in 1940, and raised her kids there, too. One time, I was telling her about my teen friend Bobby, a Maui local whose dad was haole and mom was Japanese. "Oh," Edie said about Bobby, "Then he's hapa." In all the years I'd spent on Maui when I was a teenager—and all the years I'd spent on Kaua'i as an adult—I'd somehow never heard the term. When I asked her what it meant, Edie explained, "Half Asian, half Caucasian." The full term is hapa-haole, but most people just say hapa.

There was a lot I could relate to in this concept: being half one thing, half another. I'm half Italian, half Irish. But I'm also adopted, so I'm half nature (my unknown biological parents), and half nurture (the mom and dad who raised me). By the time Edie said the word "hapa" to me, I also had a well-developed case of vitiligo, an auto-immune condition that kills off the color in my skin in patches. So half my body was still olive brown and capable of turning a deep tan, while the other half was white white and could only burn.

One thing I learned in all the years I'd spent on Maui as a teenager and all the years I'd spent on Kaua'i as an adult is that Hawaiian words and their meanings are not for mainlanders to take and bend to our own needs. We'd done enough of that already. So it's not like I went around referring to myself as hapa. I just carried that word in my heart.

Not everyone who discovered the word hapa kept it to themselves. Tyra Banks did a "hapa-inspired" photo shoot on *America's Next Top Model* where the contestants posed as racial mixes like Moroccan-Russian, Japanese-Malagasy,

Batswana-Polynesian, and Mexican-Greek, and the white models wore actual blackface (WTF?). NPR has done numerous stories on the identity politics and true meaning of hapa, and who is allowed to use the term. A "Wikipedia war" (I shit you not) rages over the entry for hapa. It started with some mainland haole—who later admitted to knowing nothing about Hawai'i or Hawaiian culture— writing the majority of the page and claiming that hapa means mixed race *anything*, anywhere, and that the term is widely used in the Eastern US. He was confronted by a part-Native Hawaiian/part-haole who claimed that *his* racial mix is the correct and true definition of the word. Then a Honolulu local jumped in and said that's not true, it means half haole, half Asian, as my friend Edie said. This debate goes on and on and never really comes to any *right* conclusion.

I'm not laying out all this nomenclature to be purposefully confusing. I'm laying all this out to make two points: First, that taxonomy—naming—is important to humans in general, but especially in Hawai'i, where the people have been in a constant struggle to hang on to who they are and what is theirs. Second, that despite orchid leis and papaya-orange sunsets and warm Pacific waves and tiki glasses of pineapple-adorned mai tais, a lot about Hawai'i is quite complex. A lot of it is divided. A lot about Hawai'i is hard to name.

Da Kine | 'Āina

THE ENGLISH WORD "LAND" HAS PROTO-GERMANIC roots, originally meaning "a defined piece of the earth that is owned by an individual or a nation." 'Āina, the Hawaiian word for land, translates to "that which feeds us." Hawaiians traditionally believed that everything necessary for life came from the land or the sea. In return, they cared for and nurtured the land, a principle called malama 'āina. If you take from the land, you give back to the land. The land does not belong to us, but we belong to it. It's easy to see how quickly this ideology could fall apart when confronted with people accustomed to the Western concept of land as something one owns—not just to feed their family, but to amass money and power.

Prior to the mid-nineteenth century, private property wasn't even a thing in Hawai'i. The monarchy controlled all land, and the commoners (maka'āinana) lived on and took care of it. The Great Māhele, which redistributed Hawai'i's land, changed everything. In 1848, King Kamehameha III reallocated all lands previously controlled by the monarchy, dividing them between the king, the government, the ali'i (chiefs), and maka'āinana. Maka'āinana could apply to own the land they'd been living and working on. Sounds great, right? Small problem: the concept of private land ownership was totally unfamiliar to most of them, so they had no idea why they should do that. Plus, the process was incredibly complicated (aloha, bureaucracy!), and literacy was necessary to file a claim. PLUS, doing so required enough money to survey the land, and they mostly lived a sustenance farming lifestyle and weren't flush with cash. PLUS, there was a really short window of time for doing all this and getting from some rural pasture on Kaua'i, for instance, to Honolulu was not an easy feat. In the long run, of the 1,523,000 acres available, only 28,658 went to the people of Hawai'i.

Part Two of the Great Māhele was the Kuleana Act of 1850, which allowed the government to sell unclaimed land to the next interested party—including foreigners. Those folks wasted no time. By May 1850, two-thirds of Hawai'i was owned by outsiders. On top of that, when the monarchy was overthrown in 1893 by white plantation owners, the property that had belonged to the king (called Crown Lands) and the government became *theirs*.

I could write a very, very long book solely on the topic of how the Hawaiians lost their land (see, for example, Jon Van Dyke's *Who Owns the Crown Lands of Hawai'i*, which clocks in at 504 pages), but it's easier to keep this one simple principle in mind: the United States and Great Britain were and are colonialists, and what colonialists do is take land from native peoples.

Bombs Away

OMBS EXPLODED SEVEN MILES AWAY. SEVEN MILES looked like a lot less at night, when the only thing between me and the bombs was a dark ribbon of ocean. The flares were like giant Roman candles streaking into the indigo sky. Sometimes the sonic booms rattled the windows on south Maui, and once an unexploded bomb landed in the Maui mayor's cow pasture. The dark ribbon of ocean protecting me from the assault was the ʻAlalākeiki Channel, the waterway separating the southwestern coast of Maui from the island of Kahoʻolawe.

I was lying on Wailea Beach with a Californian named Steve who was vacationing on Maui with his best friend's family. My brother's name was also Steve, and the way you can tell which one I'm referring to is by which one I was desperately trying to make out with. This Steve and I were smoking weed from a bong made from a Sugar Free Dr. Pepper can, weed that I'd bought from Miles, the bartender at the Luau Pool at the InterContinental Hotel.

In the early 1980s I spent a lot of time on Wailea Beach, which means I spent a lot of time watching bombs explode on Kahoʻolawe. I wouldn't call it a pastime, exactly, but the nearest mall and movie theater and Burger King were a half hour away, so if you were old enough to be out at night but not old enough to be in a bar, there's a good chance you were sitting on the beach getting high. Watching the pyrotechnics of exploding bombs seemed almost natural. Maybe even romantic.

* * *

Kahoʻolawe is the smallest of the eight major Hawaiian islands, and the only one that is uninhabited. It is dusty and dry, in the rain shadow of Mount Haleakalā, with no source of fresh water. Even before the bombing, it was hardly the verdant paradise characteristic of the emerald cliffs of Kauaʻi or the interior mountains of Oʻahu. Kahoʻolawe became an eyesore, an anomaly, an allegory, as if the "Aloha Spirit" purposefully skipped over the island and let it fall into a seventh-ring hellscape amid the galactic paradise.

* * *

Wailea is a planned resort community: hotels and swanky condos, overpriced boutiques, restaurants and golf courses built in close enough proximity to each other so that tourists won't be tempted to leave. Kīhei is where residents—kamaʻāina—actually live. Even though my dad and Steve and I always stayed at the InterContinental Hotel in Wailea, we liked to think we were more than just tourists. We had friends who lived on island. We hung out in Kīhei and wore Local Motion clothing and boogie-boarded at then-remote Makena Beach. When we had the munchies late at night, Steve and I drove to the Burger King in Kahului. Resort tourists didn't do that. We were so dead-set against being tourists that we didn't do a lot of "the things tourists do," like see the sunrise from Haleakalā, or drive the twisted road to Hana, or—god forbid—hike the jungle and mountain trails. The delusional irony, of course, was that the majority of our activities revolved around the InterContinental: volleyball on the manicured lawn, bodysurfing at the beach, and sunbathing by the Luau Pool—where Miles never served me booze, but did sell me weed that I'd smoke from a pop-can bong.

Steve was from Los Altos, funny and cute, blonde and blue-eyed, but not like a surfer or a model. Like a Northern Californian *musician*, and I had a thing for musicians. While playing volleyball on thick-blade grass that afternoon, I'd told Steve that if he could make four points in the last half of the match, I'd buy him dinner. He got the four points and I pretended to be bummed that I had to cough up dinner—as if I paid for anything. Every aspect of the vacation was bankrolled by my dad. Well, except for the weed. I paid for that with earnings from my hamburger-joint job back in Denver. Steve and I ate at the Lanai Terrace— which we just called "the coffee shop"—where he had a Monte Cristo sandwich and I had a shrimp Louis salad. Afterwards, we went to the beach to get stoned and watch the stars and the bombs.

"You know what, Steve?" I said into the dark.

"What?" His voice was all dreamy-high.

I said it in one long sentence without any pauses. "This probably isn't a great time to bring this up but I'm really relaxed so I figure what the hell I really like you a lot and want to get together with you before you leave."

He laughed a laugh I couldn't discern back then, but now I totally get to mean: *Where the hell did that come from?* "Wow."

"And if you have a brain, you'd have already figured that out by now."

We listened to the bombs. We watched the flares across the channel. High-powered gunfire sparked in the dark as the headlights of military vehicles climbed the island's desolate terrain. The island was desolate because decades of bombing practice by the US military had devastated the already-struggling vegetation, the wildlife, the sacred temples and ancient Hawaiian artifacts. Yes, the United States—that's who was bombing the life out of Kahoʻolawe seven miles away, as Steve and I sat in a silence that wasn't awkward only because of the Maui Wowie and the bombs.

"I'd say yes," Steve said, as if I'd asked a straightforward question, "But I don't know if it's because I'm fried and if I'll feel differently in the morning. How do you think you'll feel in the morning?"

"I'll feel the same," I said. "I've been wanting to do something about this for a while."

A "while" was six days, which is when Steve and his friends first got on my radar. I'd been in Maui for almost three weeks. When you're sixteen, almost three weeks is a painfully long time to not be with friends. I hadn't seen much of Bobby, our friend from Kīhei. He sometimes worked his dad's concession stand selling sunglasses and tanning lotion at the Luau Pool, and a couple years earlier we all started hanging out—him, me, my brother, and then Bobby's cousin, Donald. As an employee at the hotel, as a *local*, Bobby wasn't supposed to swim in the pools or play volleyball on the lawn or hang out in the lobby, but he had become our perpetual guest. Everyone at the hotel knew Bobby was with us. But on this trip, he and Donald has been subsumed by my brother, and I was left alone.

I was desperate for some connection. More than anything, I was desperate to like a guy who liked me back. I thought I'd solved that problem with Chris, this gorgeous guy from Dallas I'd met a week earlier. I saw him while playing volleyball, and that night we ran into each other at the Lanai Terrace. He told me he hated eating alone. "Do you want company?" I'd asked. After dinner we went driving with some guys he'd met at the hotel. The night was warm and smelled like plumeria and orchids, and I couldn't believe I was in a car with this beautiful boy. I don't know where or how our conversation took the turn, but it somehow arrived at him saying, "The locals here hate white people."

At that exact moment, my brother was with Bobby and Donald. Locals.

"Most of the white people treat them like trash," I said, and by white people I meant tourists with money.

"Well, they are trash," Chris said in his Dallas drawl.

Did he notice how I didn't speak again? We weren't high, and there were no bombs or stars to focus on. Just me checking out, wanting to be anywhere but with this guy.

When we pulled into the hotel parking lot, my brother was just getting out of our family's rental car a few rows over. "He was probably taking Bobby and Donald home," I said to Chris.

"I didn't mean to cut down your friends," he said. "I mean, they seem nice, but most of the locals are just scum."

When we got inside the lobby, Chris's friends peeled off, leaving us alone. He asked me to hang out at the Central Pool with him, and he didn't mean for a swim. He meant just him and me lying on lounge chairs next to the clear blue water, underneath the tropical stars, kissing.

"I don't think I'll be able to make it," I said.

He looked surprised. He honestly didn't see this moment coming? "Well, maybe I'll see you before I leave tomorrow morning."

"I probably won't be awake," I said, and went back to my room, despondent, wondering why this was the only guy I could attract, but the guys I really liked never worked out.

"I guess I could say I'm losing faith," I wrote in my journal, *"but that would be a lie, because I've already lost it."*

* * *

The story of Kahoʻolawe is the story of a family's black sheep. It is the hard-living addict the family has tried to help time and time again, passed from relative to relative as each one grew depleted, sometimes helping, but often making things worse.

Twelve different people held leases to Kahoʻolawe between 1858 and 1909. They brought in sheep and goats that overgrazed the land, they tried to get rid of sheep and goats that overgrazed the land. They planted trees to stop the topsoil from blowing away. They brought over cows and more sheep and suffered through severe droughts. The governor designated Kahoʻolawe a Territorial Forest Reserve, hoping to replenish the island, but replenishing the island required eliminating the feral sheep and goat population—a mass extermination that (once again) proved impossible. Forest Reserve status was revoked. A Wyoming cowboy named Angus McPhee was granted a 21-year lease. He wanted to raise cattle, but was legally required to eradicate the sheep and goats within four years. McPhee managed to slaughter, capture, or sell over twelve thousand goats and sheep in two years. Although it wasn't the entire population, it was more than anyone else had accomplished, so the territorial governor extended McPhee's lease until 1953, at which time the land would, theoretically, be returned to Hawaiʻi.

On December 7, 1941, martial law was declared in Hawaiʻi and control of the island was taken away from Angus McPhee. It was supposed to be returned to him (and eventually to Hawaiʻi) after WWII, but the US decided Kahoʻolawe was too perfect a place to simulate war. They loved that they could bombard the island with shore fire *and* ground fire *and* air fire at the same time. Perhaps this was doable on other Pacific islands, but Kahoʻolawe's proximity to Pearl Harbor (a mere 100 hundred miles) probably made it easier and cheaper to bomb the hell out of than some atoll in the middle of Micronesia (two thousand+ miles). And we had to test bombs—to practice war—somewhere, right?

This is the story of Kahoʻolawe: drought, sheep, goats, and then war, which led to bombs. By the way: bombing the island turned out to be one of the more effective solutions for thinning the herds. Not that it was the primary goal. Just a fringe benefit.

* * *

Two days after ditching the racist guy from Dallas, I met Steve, which led to us lying on the beach not talking about the fact that this island in front of us was being bombed. Even though we were from the mainland, somehow the violence seemed perfectly normal.

"What are you thinking about?" I asked him.

"Well, what about Evan?" Evan was his best friend's older brother—and by older, I mean eighteen. "I think he likes you."

I'd on-and-off wondered the same thing, every day going back and forth between "I think he likes me" to "He just likes me as a friend." The word *like* had so many nuances at that age.

Steve and I turned on our sides, not seeing the flares or the stars anymore, just each other. "He wasn't sure if he was supposed to make the first move," he said.

Evan was nice enough, I guess, and not bad-looking, but I just didn't feel *that* way about him. "Do you like me?" I asked Steve.

"Yes."

"As more than a friend?"

"I think *so*." He emphasized *so*, not *think*, which mattered to my stony brain. Of course, teenage stony brains are reliably unreliable.

I moved my hand to his head and played with his wavy blonde hair, bleached out by the saltwater and

chlorine and tropical sun. I kissed his forehead, then
his cheek, then next to—but not on—his lips, giving
him plenty of time to pull away if he wanted. It didn't
occur to me that maybe there was something wrong
with having to work this hard to get him to kiss me. Or
maybe there wasn't. Even now, over thirty years later, I
don't understand the motivations of teenage boys. We're
told it's sex, then more sex, and then even more sex, but
I also know they can care about people and doing the
right thing. Not all of them get together with a girl just
because she's present and willing.

I kissed Steve's chapped lips, and he kissed back. I
had no awareness of the booms or flares or bright lights
across the channel, of the Navy literally bombing the life
out of this island that was settled by Polynesians in 400
CE, that was ruled by violent chiefs, that became a colony
where criminals were sent into exile, that was overrun by
feral animals, that was stolen from the Hawaiian people.
In 1981—two years before I was making out with Steve—
Kahoʻolawe had been added to the Register of National
Historic Places in hopes of saving whatever remained
of the sacred religious sites and ancient artifacts and
petroglyphs carved into lava rock. But the destruction
continued. The island was a metaphor for a metaphor for
the real deal.

I asked Steve how he's feeling now.

"Better," he said. "Not so stoned."

"Are you still unsure about this?" I asked.

"No, I'm sure," he said, and we kissed again. I wondered
how he'd feel in the morning.

* * *

In the mid-1970s, Kahoʻolawe became ground zero for the Hawaiian Renaissance, a movement to restore Native culture. An activist group called "Protect Kahoʻolawe ʻOhana" (sometimes shortened to PKO, sounding too much like a terrorist group for me) staged a series of illegal landings on the island. During their first "access," as they called it, ʻOhana members discovered the remnants of ancient fishing villages and religious temples. They also saw an island that was dying—just like the Hawaiian culture.

The ʻOhana group grew and strengthened under the guiding principle of aloha ʻāina: love for the land and a responsibility to protect it. They lobbied the state legislature and flew to Washington, DC to request federal support. They filed a lawsuit against the Department of Defense, demanding the bombing cease and the island be returned to Hawaiʻi. None of that did a bit of good, so they chose the route of civil disobedience.

In January 1977, several ʻOhana members covertly landed on Kahoʻolawe. Most of them returned to Honolulu soon after to announce that two men, Richard Sawyer and Walter Ritte, had remained on the island. Sawyer and Ritte brought enough food and water to survive for two weeks. Three weeks later, one hundred marines and a fleet of helicopters were dispatched to track them down. Sawyer and Ritte managed to evade the military, and their occupation stretched out to a month. At that point, they decided to give themselves up. The problem was, the military had lost interest. They even *resumed bombing* and, amid the chaos, Ritte and Sawyer couldn't get their attention. They lit bonfires and flashed mirrors to send signals but, as I can attest from my adolescent perch on the coast of Maui, that wouldn't stand out from the bombings.

It was up to the 'Ohana to rescue their own. George Helm, Kimo Mitchell, and Billy Mitchell (no relation) made landing on Kaho'olawe on March 5 to search for their friends. The powerboat driver who ferried them over was supposed to retrieve them the next day, but didn't show up due to weirdly unspecified "boat problems." The three men spent two days trying to find Sawyer and Ritte, to no avail. With limited supplies and the ongoing bombing, they decided it best to hightail it over to Maui via the two surfboards they'd brought. About halfway across the rough 'Alalākeiki Channel, Billy Mitchell lost sight of George and Kimo. The winds and currents were so powerful that it made more sense for him to retreat to Kaho'olawe—where he ran the risk of being blown up or arrested—than to continue towards Maui. Upon landing, Billy immediately located the Marines and told them of his missing friends. The otherwise-at-odds 'Ohana and US military joined forces to search for them, but George Helm and Kimo Mitchell were never found. Officially lost at sea.

I don't find their deaths the most surprising part of the story. Maybe that's what comes of being born in 1967, with the background of race riots and the Vietnam War entering your cellular memory. What surprises me most is that, of all the accounts I read, none revealed the fate of the men Helm and Mitchell went to rescue. It wasn't until I unearthed an Appeal of the Ninth Circuit

Court reviewing Ritte and Sawyers' arrest and six-month imprisonment that I discovered the military had located and removed them from Kahoʻolawe on March 5—the very day their ill-fated friends arrived to save them.

* * *

It was late morning at the same beach where Steve and I made out the night before. He was out snorkeling with his best friend. It was cloudy, and not the way it often is in the Islands—fluffy clouds moving from mountain to shore and shore to mountain, maybe releasing a quick shower—but was a portent of real rain. The kind that keeps tourists indoors, confused and unsure about how to pass their time. Across the choppy channel Kahoʻolawe was dormant. No flares or booms, just convalescence.

Steve emerged from the water. I don't know if I asked how the snorkeling was, but I assume it must have been shitty. Cloudy like the skies. Steve and I sat on the sand, our long gaze towards Kahoʻolawe. Without the dark and without the weed, I wasn't as bold, so it took me a while to screw up the courage to say, "I've just got to ask…now that it's morning, how do you feel?"

"No differently," he said.

The day went on as usual: swimming, lunch, volleyball, dinner with my dad and brother, and then, that night, getting stoned on the beach again with Steve.

"Did you like last night?" he asked me. God, the amount of reassurance we needed at that age.

"Yeah," I said. "Did you?"

"Oh, *yeah*," he said.

I asked him if he thought I was easy because I'd been so forward, and he said no. But five minutes later he asked, "Do you try to get together with every blond musician you meet?"

I thought about it for a long time, some might suggest too long, but since we were high the passage of time wasn't relevant. I tried to recall the number of blond musicians I'd met in my *vast* dating life of about a year and a half. I couldn't think of anyone other than Steve. "No," I said. "He'd have to be unique."

My guess is that by "unique" I meant he'd have to be cute and funny, as well as a blond musician—although I'm not even sure why that, "blond musician," was a metric. Maybe there was something about the Police and David Bowie and Nick Rhodes populating MTV in 1983 that put an extra premium on blonds. Maybe it's why I'd kissed brown eyed, black-haired Bobby the summer before, but never again. Maybe that's why he didn't hang out with me anymore.

"Okay then," Steve said. "I don't think you're easy."

To be clear—because it might be important to you or maybe just to me—all we did was make out. There was no excessive rubbing or caressing, no undressing, no climaxing. Just kissing. Connection.

That summer I spent three-and-a-half weeks on Maui, and the most important relationship I thought I could have was with a boy. Not to the 'āina, the land, or to the host culture I so frivolously consumed. I've since learned to connect to both earthly and heavenly elements in infinite ways—land, sky, water, bodies, my own heart. But at that age, connection required male affection as the conduit—to my own body, my own heart, even to the land I sat on and saw being destroyed before my eyes.

* * *

The bombing of Kahoʻolawe continued until 1990, and then it took another four years until control of the island was returned to Hawaiʻi. It would be nice to think Kahoʻolawe was some sort of anomaly, a cautionary tale from which a valuable lesson is learned and heeded, but 20 percent of the state's land is still controlled by the military. That's over one hundred installations on two hundred and thirty-six thousand acres, from the Pacific Missile Range Facility on West Kauaʻi to the Big Island's Pohakuloa Training Area, to the granddaddy of them all: Pearl Harbor. Between direct Department of Defense expenditures and the spending of military families, it's estimated that the military presence contributes over $14.7 billion a year to Hawaiʻi's economy, making it second only to tourism in its economic impact. And, like tourism, while the military has helped the Islands flourish financially, it has also devastated its culture.

Scores of unexploded ordnance still litter Kahoʻolawe, some buried out of sight, some protruding up in the air. Volunteers work cautiously and tirelessly to clean up and restore the island. When I recently returned to Maui for the first time in twenty-three years, my plane flew by Kahoʻolawe. I was alone, my husband back home, my entire family ashes in urns. Kahoʻolawe was no longer pockmarked and brown. My breath caught. Greenery laid in a smooth blanket over the land. I slowly released the air trapped in my chest, whispering, "My god." The island looked healthy, alive, but I knew that which is destroyed cannot be brought back. What is gone will always be gone.

Da Kine | Kama'āina

KAMA'ĀINA LITERALLY TRANSLATES TO "CHILD OF THE land," and means a permanent resident of Hawai'i. It's one of the few identifiers in Hawai'i that has nothing to do with ethnic background or skin color. Anyone who lives in the state as a permanent resident—haole, hapa, Hawaiian, or otherwise—can claim title as kama'āina. (And no, having a vacation home in Hawai'i doesn't count. Your driver's license has gotta have a Hawai'i address on it.) Discounts at hotels, restaurants, and stores are offered to kama'āina, since it's recognized that prices are inflated for tourism. This can range from getting a free appetizer with an entrée, to 50 percent off nightly hotel rates.

In 1976, a Californian named Marybelle Archibald brought a class-action lawsuit against several Hawaiian hotels for offering kama'āina rates. She claimed the local discount constituted "unlawful discrimination" against her and violated the "constitutional rights under equal protection, privileges, and immunities" of people who weren't residents, like herself. It's a good thing this happened forty years ago and that I can't find Ms. Archibald on Facebook, because I pretty much want to slap her upside the head. Mostly, I like to imagine all the cross-lawsuits this could spur, where Native Hawaiians sue the United States and Great Britain and Australia and Holland for all the ways they've been discriminated against since Western contact.

Ms. Archibald's lawsuit—and all its appeals— was dismissed.

Reverend Jim's Ten Commandments for Growing Up Haole on Oʻahu

A FTER HER HUSBAND DIED IN 1973, EDIE JONES moved her haole kids from rural Nebraska to Oʻahu, where she grew up. Edie told me that of all her kids, the one who most wanted to be Native Hawaiian was her oldest, Jim. He didn't want to be a colonialist or a tourist or a haole, someone who came to the Islands and took, someone who came from nowhere. Maybe it's because his dad died when he was six and he just wanted to belong, to be a part of something that could and would survive.

A surfer and journeyman musician, Jim has been known by several names throughout his life: JJ, Rockstar, JimJones (all one word), James Eliot Jones, and Reverend Jim. Jim is thin, with long brown hair that he often wears in two braids, a floppy brown mustache and graying goatee, and tattoos up and down his arms.

I asked Reverend Jim what it was like growing up haole in Honolulu (or Honolulu-adjacent), and he spoke these words:

1. **I am white, not haole**, and I have to keep proving that I'm not haole all the time. I'm totally cool with that. You shall have no anger that you're blamed for the shitty things other haoles have done. You may think you didn't do anything—and so you shouldn't have to prove anything—but your granddad, or your grand-dad's best friend, or some other asshole stole the islands from the Hawaiians, he stole their culture and their religion and their land.

2. **You shall not forget that haole can mean different things** at different times, and you don't get to define it. It's all about context. A local might yell, "Hey haole boy! What's up?" with a smile, or "Fucking haole, keep your fucking shitty haole bitch off this fucking beach" (without a smile). The haole thing is hard, because it can be whatever locals want it to be. But it's not really about the color of your skin. It doesn't mean white person—it means "other." It just means, "you're not like us." So if you *are* like them, then you're not haole.

3. **You shall not disrespect the local people** and their culture. This is about surfing, about Hawaiian culture, about society. Hawai'i is super tribal. Show deference. You have to give respect, straight out, and you have to earn it.

4. **Remember that in Hawai'i** people are raised to be super straight and not sugarcoat the truth. If you only say what you think people want to hear, especially if you're a guy, you're the biggest asshole the world's ever

seen. Guys from the Southern US tend to hate living in Hawai'i for this reason. If you tell a bandmate from the South to fuck off, he'll set down his guitar and never play with you again. In Hawai'i, guys get in fist fights at rehearsal, then all go to the bar and do shots together afterwards.

5. **Honor the water.** Don't show up at Sunset or Pipeline for the first time and smoke a joint and just jump into the ocean with your board because you've surfed in California or North Carolina or somewhere other than Hawai'i, and think you know what you're doing. Watch the ocean. Watch the waves, watch the currents for an hour, for two hours. Understand how they move—which is really fast. And that's just the regular current, not the rip currents. The regular currents are so strong you have to constantly paddle just to stay in one place. If you stop paddling, you're suddenly three miles down the beach and someone has to rescue you with two hundred other people in the water.

6. **You shall not speed** and honk your horn in traffic. If you do this on the Pali Highway, for instance, there's a chance a big local guy in big pickup truck will force you to the side of the road, get out of his car and lean in your window and say right in your face, "Hey, brah, where you going so fast?" And when you tell him where you're going, he'll say, "What, not going to be there when you get there?" and when you concede that yes, it will most likely be there no matter when you get

there, he'll say, "Well, then slow the fuck down, yeah?"
and get back in his truck and drive away.

7. **You shall not show fear when you're confronted by
   locals**. If you're afraid, you're fucked. Eye contact is a
   thing. You've got to make a little eye contact, but then
   you've gotta look away. Because if you hold eye contact,
   that's considered staring and means you want to fight.
   But if you won't look at 'em, it means you're afraid. And
   why are you afraid of them?

8. **You shall not walk away from a fight** with locals. If you
   do, you cannot have any kind of life. They will confront
   you nearly every week of your life—even when you are
   seven years old, on your first day at 'Aikahi Elementary
   School—and when you fight back they will laugh and
   call you lolo haole and chase you around and hit you
   some more. But if you don't fight back, you cannot
   hang with the locals, you cannot date those girls, you
   cannot go surfing in those places, you cannot go to
   those parties, you cannot play in bands with those guys.
   You cannot have a life.

9. **You shall not be fatherless**, even if your father died
   when you were six years old. One friend's big brother
   will teach you to sail, and another friend's father will
   teach you to tie knots and fix a dingy. Another friend's
   grandfather will teach you how to lay down fishing
   nets. Your mother will take in two teenage girls whose
   mother died and whose father is unable to care for

them. They start hanging around your house after giving you a ride back from guitar camp, and never leave. Your mom never questions that she's now housing and feeding children who are not hers. There's a Hawaiian word for this, nurturing other people's kids: hānai. It's not a legal arrangement, and it isn't a paid service, and it isn't done out of obligation. Hānai is done out of love.

10. **You shall not be a teenage pothead wannabe-rock star** and expect a father to be cool when you impregnate his 17-year-old part-Hawaiian daughter. He is Muscogee Creek, 6'4" and 260 pounds, and rumored to have killed a man on the mainland in the sixties. You have been with the girl since she was 14, and at first her Father hated you mostly because you were both too young. He is not like the other men, the hānai who see you have no father and try to fill that role. This Father sees the path you are on, the path that being a rock star wannabe in the early eighties often leads to (coke, heroin, jail). His concern is protecting his daughter, this precious mix of Native Hawaiian and Native American blood, and his grandson, the first male born into their bloodline in generations. Right before you leave Hawai'i for LA (so you can become a rock star bigger than Axl Rose), the Father will attack you at a Burger King and you will say "Fuck you," because this is how you are. How you fight. How you have fought since your first day at 'Aikahi Elementary School. After you leave Hawai'i, you do go down the

path the Father saw you on (coke, heroin, jail), so you are no longer allowed to see your son. And when your son has a daughter, you shall not be allowed to see your granddaughter either. Not until you get clean, and not until the Father is dead, and not until your son is also dead from an overdose at the age of 23, when the sleeves of his Native Hawaiian tattoo, hand-tapped onto his skin with animal bones and kukui ash, are only halfway done.

Da Kine: 'Ohana

'OHANA IS THE HAWAIIAN WORD FOR FAMILY, AND yet I don't understand what it really means. It can mean biological family, and it can mean adopted family. 'Ohana can refer to the extended family systems we create for ourselves, the people who we choose to nurture us. It is a guiding principle that means to take care of each other, above all else. It is a term businesses use to refer to their employees ("Looking for part-time dishwashers to join our 'ohana!") or their customers ("It is our goal to make you feel like 'ohana."). It is an acronym for the Optical Hawaiian Array for Nanoradian Astronomy project at the Mauna Kea Observatory on the Big Island. It is the brand name of a faux-rubber/vegan slipper for men sold by the shoe company OluKai. It is the name of a tiki restaurant in Disney World's Polynesian Village where children can eat scrambled eggs and Mickey Mouse waffles for $20 while being visited by Lilo and Stitch. It is the name of a 'ukulele manufacturer, several wicker furniture stores, a chartered yacht, a hotel, a real-estate developer, a surf shop, a Baptist church, a new-age wellness center, a hair salon, a photography studio, a brand of fruit punch, an organic laundry service, a radio media group, and more restaurants than I can begin to count.

'Ohana means so many things that I wonder if it truly means anything anymore.

Descendant(s)

O N A WARM JANUARY EVENING IN 2012, MY HUSBAND Michael and I lay on the bed of our Līhuʻe hotel room watching *The Descendants*. It was our first viewing, even though the movie had been out for two months and nominated for five Academy Awards. It's weird we hadn't seen it yet for two reasons: one, because I'm obsessed with Hawaiʻi, where *The Descendants* takes place, and usually consume any and everything to do with it, and two, because, duh, George Clooney.

This scene was doubly weird because we were staying in a hotel in Līhuʻe in the first place. Līhuʻe is the administrative capital of Kauaʻi, home to the island's only commercial airport. Līhuʻe is where you can depend on having to wait in a line—at your hotel, at a restaurant, to rent a boogie board, to find a parking space, to eventually make a left turn. It's where cruise ships dock and shuttle passengers to Kmart to buy cheap macadamia nuts and tiki shot glasses and Kona coffee. Līhuʻe is crowded and loud by Kauaʻi standards, so we always stay in Poʻipū, fifteen miles away. But that January afternoon, we had arrived at the Līhuʻe Marriott after abandoning the house we were renting in Poʻipū because the windows in the house either didn't open or didn't close, and all of them had signs warning us to keep them locked, otherwise burglary was likely. We abandoned the house because there was a milky-white stain on the comforter, and even after we moved it to another room, I couldn't get rid of the icks. The side of the refrigerator was covered in rust, and the bathroom faucet and tiles were covered in scale. The couch was both too hard and too soft, and was made of some waterproof, sunscreen-proof fabric that made me itch. We abandoned the house because the second we walked in—before I knew about the windows or the rust or the comforter or the itch—I immediately sensed bad juju. Some messy weightedness that had been left there by a previous guest or the owners that didn't belong to me and that I couldn't fend off. I wasn't strong enough. I needed to be coddled, comforted, secure.

Five months earlier my bipolar brother, Steve, had suffered two fatal pulmonary emboli in the middle of the night, fourteen months after our dad died. Steve was forty-five. I flew from Portland to Denver for his funeral, held on what would have been my mom's seventy-fifth birthday, if my mom were still alive. Three weeks later I returned to Denver and, in one long weekend, cleaned out the house I grew up in, the house Steve and my dad shared. It was four thousand square feet of detritus collected by two small-time hoarders over forty-five years. My childhood home was in foreclosure because my dad died with massive debt, and it would be auctioned off by the city. I came to Hawai'i only a month out of the subsequent—almost unavoidable—nervous breakdown that almost took me away from this world.

That's why my husband and I were staying at a hotel in Līhu'e.

The Descendants begins with a montage of real life in Honolulu: high-rises, freeway traffic, homelessness, and an old woman reaching up to rub her neck as if trying to rid herself of a deep ache. George Clooney's character, Matt King, narrates that mainlanders assume he lives in some sort of perpetual paradise where nothing bad happens, where people feel no pain or sickness or suffering simply because they are surrounded by palms trees and waves. He ends the speech with five glorious words: "Paradise can go fuck itself."

The Descendants is based on a novel of the same name by Kaui Hart Hemmings. While adapting it for the screen, Alexander Payne emotionally condensed the story—as one must do when turning a 283-page novel into a 127-page screenplay. Some of the material jettisoned makes total sense, scenes and lines that weren't necessary to tell the larger story. Some changes were more puzzling: the name of Matt's wife, for instance, was changed from Joanie to Elizabeth. But Payne nonetheless remained loyal to what the story is about. First, it is about an immediate family: Matt and his wife Elizabeth (in the movie), their teen daughter Alexandra, and their ten-year-old daughter Scottie. When the movie starts, the family is scattered in vastly different directions emotionally and, in some cases, geographically. Matt is immersed in his work and hasn't emotionally engaged with Elizabeth for so long that, he later finds out, she's been having an affair. Alex is a problem teen—drinking, drugs, bad grades, and we assume sex—and has been sent to boarding school on the Big Island to straighten her out. Ten-year-old Scottie cusses, watches porn with her friends, and bullies other kids at school.

And then Elizabeth suffers a speed boating accident that puts her in a permanent coma. Her living will mandates she not be kept alive artificially, so Matt is legally required to pull the plug. This already-fractured family must figure out some way to come together and deal with the new fracture. This permanent fracture, the one that cannot be fixed.

A counselor told me that when my mom died, my family went from being a table with four legs to a table with three legs. Maybe, in some families, the remaining three legs try to compensate for the missing fourth. My family didn't do that. We pretended that fourth leg wasn't missing, or wasn't that important, or that we weren't even one table, since my parents were divorced and Steve and I were both technically "adults" (twenty-eight and twenty-six, respectively). It felt like my mom and I had been one table, Steve and my dad the other, and I had to deal with the brokenness on my own. But less than ten years after my mom died, the systemic instability became apparent, and we all started to fall down. My brother's mental illness led to severe physical illness, and my dad, unable to deal with the consequences, repeatedly tried to commit suicide. And then there was me, trying not to implode while my remaining family did.

The Descendants is also about family on a bigger scale: Matt's great-great grandmother was a Hawaiian princess, one of the last descendants of King Kamehameha the Great. She married her haole banker, and together the power couple amassed thousands of acres of land. As a result, Matt and his extended family own twenty-five thousand acres of undeveloped property on Kaua'i that sits in a trust. The extended family is referred to as "The Cousins"—there are no parents in Matt's family, no aunts or uncles or siblings, and certainly no grandparents. Just like me at the age of forty-four.

While Elizabeth is lying in this permanent coma, The Cousins are days away from voting on who to sell their twenty-five thousand acres to because a law dictates that, in seven years, the trust holding the land be dissolved. While the book doesn't cite a legal reason for the trust being dissolved—it's more focused on the financial drain the taxes has on the family—Payne and a law scholar he engaged saw this as an opportunity to provide some poignant Hawaiian history. Randall Roth, a professor at the University of Hawai'i, advised Payne of the Rule Against Perpetuities, which states that a private trust must be dissolved twenty-one years after the last person involved in the creation of the trust dies. (This is apparently an incredibly convoluted law, so I'm just giving the headlines here.) In general, the Rule Against Perpetuities is meant to limit how long descendants must abide by a dead person's wishes. The law is particularly relevant in Hawai'i, where vast amounts of land were acquired by the white aristocracy in the 1800s. The RAP means, in theory, that imperialist sugar barons and pineapple barons and sandalwood barons don't get to control Hawaiian land forever.

Most of Matt King's cousins haven't exactly been out there making a living and are depending on this eventual sale as their cash cow. Matt only lives off the money he earns as a lawyer, so that's not his concern. He's also the sole trustee and can basically do whatever he wants. There's tremendous pressure on him to make the "right" decision—not just from The Cousins, but also from the residents of Hawai'i, who have an emotional investment, a spiritual investment, in what happens to this enormous unspoiled parcel of beach and jungle and pasture. Many people don't want him to sell at all, because they don't want to see more shopping malls and golf courses and hotels and condos and traffic on their island paradise. Wherever Matt goes, people ask, "Do you know what you're going to do yet?"

If there is one fault to the movie plot, it would have to be that seven years doesn't seem like the most urgent ticking clock in the world. My dad was a real estate developer and named eleven heirs in his will so, trust me, I understand the complications of dividing things like land and stocks among numerous parties. I get that in trying to distribute twenty-five thousand acres of land equitably, someone will inevitably feel ripped off because they didn't get the beachfront location, or the land with the great view, or whatever signals "value" to them. But I have a hard time believing that a decision that will not only affect the financial solvency of Matt's twenty-four slacker cousins, but also the *entire state* of Hawai'i, has to be made at the exact moment his wife is being taken off life support.

Elizabeth is on life support for the entire movie, except for an opening scene shot without music or dialogue that shows her speeding through the ocean in a powerboat. You only see her from the chest up, giving the sense that she's levitating. Honolulu and Diamond Head are in the background, getting farther and farther away from Elizabeth with each second. She doesn't just look happy in this short scene; she looks content. A few times in my life I have thought, "I could die right now and I'd be happy"—like when I saw the Eiffel Tower light up and sparkle at night. But in times when I have felt content, when my body and soul feel at rest—usually when I am near an ocean, the Pacific Ocean, Kaua'i—I want to stay in that place forever. Although Elizabeth is depicted as some sort of thrill-seeker, that's not what the opening scene tells me. She wanted to feel wanted by the world, to belong to it. It's why she's having an affair. It's why she's speeding on a boat with the sun and saltwater spraying her face.

Except for during that short whiff of contentedness, we only see Elizabeth in a hospital bed, in a coma, her breathing labored, her eyes closed. When my mom was in a coma, her eyes were open, sort of rolled back into her head. At one point, a kind nurse closed them. She also dotted Vaseline on my mom's lips. As Elizabeth nears death, rolled-up washcloths are placed in her fists to keep her hands from contorting into claws and digging into her own palms. My mom never had the washcloths, because it was only 24 hours between when she slipped into the coma and when she died. For Elizabeth King, it was almost a month.

Not surprisingly, several parties are interested in the King family's 25K acres. One of the leading bids is from a Chicago developer who has offered an astounding half a billion dollars. There's another bid from a guy named Holitzer that isn't for quite as much—but still reasonable—and is favorable because he's from Kaua'i. Sort of. He's a Kaua'i-born haole who went on to make a fortune in Silicon Valley, an allusion to AOL cofounder Steve Case, who was born in Honolulu and now owns forty thousand acres on Kaua'i. Most of The Cousins want to sell to Holitzer, the slightly smaller bid, because at least the ownership and money comes from and "stays in state." This is *kind of* conscientious, and shows *sort of* an understanding of the complexity of outside ownership. Never mind that Holitzer is haole, not Hawaiian, and still intends to build resorts and golf courses, and very well might hire mainland developers to do so. But The Cousins' perspective represents a very real one for many residents of Hawai'i—haole and otherwise: the land is there, tourism is a major industry, lots of money is nice to have, so why not just rip up the kukui and koa and monkeypod trees?

Like the Northern Spotted Owl became a symbol of deforestation in the Pacific Northwest, the monkeypod tree is the poster child for the political, cultural, and environmental concerns surrounding tourist development on Kaua'i. Old Kōloa Town, adjacent to the resort community of Po'ipū, is lined with shops and restaurants in original plantation buildings that have been restored and renovated. The area was long known for the forty monkeypod trees providing a great canopy of shade for the buildings.

Then, in 2008, a Michigan developer called The Nelsen Companies moved ahead on a plan to build a Brand! New! Strip! Mall! in Old Kōloa Town. Their first step was bulldozing seventeen historic monkeypod trees. Locals weren't happy. *We* weren't happy—and we're tourists, for godsake. But we're the kind of tourists who go to Hawai'i to get away from strip malls, who don't want to see the character of an historic town decimated for redundant retail outlets. (The tenants committed to the Shops at Kōloa included a grocery store—even though there is one 250 feet in one direction and another five hundred feet in the other direction; an American Savings Bank, even though First Hawaiian Bank is just down the block; a shave ice store, even though there's already one around the corner...you get the picture.) The most heinous of the promised tenants was an ABC, one of a chain of seventy-eight stores that sells cheap puka shell necklaces, plastic leis, printed T-shirts, cellophane grass hula skirts, calendars of bikini-clad local women, toy 'ukuleles, and pineapple-shaped serving dishes made from monkeypod wood.

There were protests before the monkeypod trees were bulldozed, and after they were bulldozed, and it seems all for naught: nine years later, absolutely no building has commenced. Construction stalled over permit and financing problems. At least two of the stores originally committed to tenancy have backed out, further obstructing the developer's ability to finance the project. It sounds like another story of a mainland developer barging in and trying to bulldoze paradise to make big bucks, until you dig a little. That's when you find that The Nelsen

Companies was simply contracted by the actual owner of the land. The owner of the land is the Eric A. Knudsen Trust. Eric A. Knudsen is a descendant of a West Kaua'i sugarcane baron who was married to Anne McHutchison Sinclair, who was the daughter of Elizabeth Sinclair, who purchased the island of Ni'ihau from King Kamehameha V for $10,000 in gold in 1864. Her descendants still own Ni'ihau and protect it as a private homeland for Native Hawaiians where there are no hotels, no stores, no paved roads, and no visitors allowed. Although Elizabeth Sinclair's descendants—and Eric Knudson's—are haole, they have lived on and protected the land, the 'āina, for 150 years. Which is to say, the people who decided to plow down those monkeypod trees to make way for an ABC Store are not mainland bad guys. They're not exactly the heroes of the story, either, but like Matt King's cousins, they have a complicated relationship to the 'āina and no clear compass dictating what to do with it.

My dad, on the other hand, *was* a mainland bad guy. His relationship to land wasn't terribly complicated: he bought land and either built on it, or held on to the land until someone else needed to build on it, and sold it to them for a profit. The reason I spent so much time in Hawai'i as a teen is because my dad was building a housing subdivision on Maui. He was another haole tearing up trees and draining precious resources and contributing to Native Hawaiians getting further away from their 'āina. It never occurred to me, not until well into adulthood, that there might be anything wrong with that. The land was there, people needed housing, and I got to go to Hawai'i two or three times a year—that's what mattered to me.

Like all good plots, *The Descendants* has a complication. In this case it's—wait for it—Matt discovering that Elizabeth's lover stands to profit greatly from the sale to Holitzer through real-estate commissions. As you might imagine, Matt is not super-psyched to put money in that guy's pocket. But he also recognizes that Holitzer's bid is a good bid, and the wish of the people he represents: The Cousins. But is that really who he represents? The camera spends a lot of time spanning over black and white photos of his ancestors, from his brown-skinned great-great Grandmother wrapped in orchid leis, to her white husband, and their increasingly white children, leading up to Matt's parents. For some inexplicable reason, none of these descendants of the Hawaiian princess married Hawaiians. The family has almost completely bred out their Hawaiian blood. And yet they own Hawaiian land.

Matt is acutely aware of that small drop of Hawaiian blood still pumping through his heart and what it connects him to. This is something I will never quite understand, since I have no connection to my blood lineage. That's how it is for people adopted during the closed-records era: we went through life legally prohibited from knowing the names of our ancestors. We have no pictures of people who look like us. Even if we do somehow manage to obtain our records, if we finally manage to find a picture of someone who looks like us, if we contact them via Facebook or email or phone or snail mail, that doesn't mean those people whose blood pumps through our hearts will want anything to do with us. It doesn't mean they will connect us to who we are descended from.

It's easy enough to say that my lineage is the ancestors of the adoptive mom and dad who raised me, of Jan and Pete Prato, but that's not how it works. DNA is powerful. Blood is powerful. It is what sustains us, feeds us, keeps us alive. DNA is what ties us to lives lived long before we were born. In the book, Matt King muses about "the complicated nature of birthrights, how they are both fortuitous and undeserved." My biological birthright made me an orphan for the first ten weeks of my life; my adopted lineage gave me a mom and a dad and a brother who succumbed to mental illness and addiction. And it also gave me privilege: the privilege to go to Hawai'i dozens of times, to forge a connection to the 'āina. I did nothing to "earn" it, just like Matt King's cousins did nothing to earn the hundreds of millions of dollars they would reap from selling their land.

In one of those coincidences that we think can only happen in movies, Matt finds out that Brian Speer, the guy Elizabeth is having an affair with, is vacationing in Kaua'i, the location of the hotly contested land. Matt takes his family to Kaua'i to track down Brian. Matt's not tracking down Brian to beat the shit out of him, but to give him the opportunity to return to O'ahu and say goodbye to Elizabeth. Okay, that stretches plausibility a little, that anyone could be *that* nice of a guy—especially one who's been essentially ignoring his wife for years. But the true suspension of disbelief is that Matt flies his daughters to another island while their mother is dying.

(Scottie, the youngest, doesn't even know that Elizabeth was removed from life support.) Matt couldn't just call the guy Elizabeth was sleeping with? No, he wants to see Brian's face. From that perspective, Matt's not such a nice guy, but an incredibly selfish guy.

You know what I did when my mother was dying? I sat by her bed. I watched *Star Trek: The Next Generation* while Steve narrated. "It's an episode with Q, Mom," he said. "One of your favorites." I called my uncle to tell him his sister was dying. I sang "What I Did for Love" from *A Chorus Line* to her. When the priest said we needed to tell her it was okay to let go, I told my mom it was okay to let go. I went home and tried to sleep. When the phone rang at 2:00 a.m. to tell me she was slipping away, I returned to the hospital. My mom got stronger as soon as we got there, so Steve and I decided maybe she couldn't die with us there. That she knew it would be too hard on us. So we each said goodbye to her and went home. When I woke up at 10:00 a.m., I called the hospital and found out there'd been no change. My best girlfriend, the only person my age I knew who'd lost a parent, took me out to lunch. We talked about death, because we could. When I got home I called the hospital and my mom was still alive, but not alive. In a coma. Never to come out. And I realized she needed me there to die. What I did was get in my car and speed across town and hope I didn't get a ticket, and I got into bed with my mom and I put my arms around her and held her until she took her last breath. Fifteen minutes—that's how long it took from when I got in bed with her, until then. The last moment. The last breath. That's what I did when my mom was dying. It's impossible to imagine being an airplane ride—no matter how short—away, walking on the beach or listening to a 'ukulele band at Tahiti Nui in Hanalei when my mom could be taking her last breath.

This is another reason that it was weird that my husband and I were watching *The Descendants* in our hotel room in Līhu'e, five months after my brother died, a year and a half after my dad died, eighteen years after my mom died, a month after I considered joining them. You'd think that watching a mom—anyone, really—die would not be that great for my mental health. But somehow it was okay. It was okay because I was in Kaua'i and I believed the land and water would take care of me. If I had watched this movie on the mainland, I would have felt bereft, cut off, separate from the 'āina where I feel most content, when my body and soul feel at rest. But in Līhu'e I knew the next day I could walk into the water and feel the sun and the wind and the salt spray against my face. I could feel alive.

Matt understands how powerful that is. The 'āina. The sand and salt and grass and kiawe trees and rusted red dirt, and he decides he doesn't want to cede it to people with no Hawaiian blood. Matt seems to get it—not just that the clues to who we are and what we should do lie in our blood. He gets that for a hundred and fifty years his white ancestors were in possession of something that does not rightly belong to them. Two hundred years earlier, the Native Hawaiian wouldn't have necessarily claimed it "belonged" to them, either. Ancient Hawaiians believed that humans belong to the land—not the other way around. It is not ours to own, but under the principle of *aloha 'āina* it's our responsibility to take care of, to nurture and protect. Matt's white ancestors changed this attitude by their very presence. Land—territory—was something they conquered and acquired.

Some scholars of Hawaiian history are quick to remind people that the kings and chiefs of the 1800s played a major role in ceding land to the white folks. Elizabeth Sinclair, for instance, didn't steal Ni'ihau from the Kingdom of Hawai'i. Kamehameha V willingly sold it to her. But just as white people brought Christianity and literacy and venereal disease to the Native Hawaiians, they also brought capitalism. They brought the idea that things— most especially land—equal power. And once capitalism inserts itself into the DNA of a culture, it's hard to go back. Many people like having the ability to acquire things to make their lives better, or more pleasurable, or whatever their metric is. Governments like having the power that producing and importing and exporting goods affords them. It's one thing if a culture has never been exposed to any of that. But as soon as the exportation of whale oil and sandalwood and sugar and pineapple became a part of the tapestry of Hawaiian life in the 1800s, it became likely that pulling out those threads would cause a great unraveling. This remains the dilemma of modern Hawai'i. Tourism has grown, and sustained, and destroyed Hawai'i. No matter how theoretically desirable reversing course may seem, it is impossible to go back.

Matt decides not to accept either of the bids, Holitzer's or the half-billion dollars—pointing out that they have seven years to figure out how to keep the land (no kidding!). While he can't exactly reverse the course of capitalism, he can stop the "progress" that keeps Hawaiians—that keeps him and his children—from the land. I have no idea what became of the subdivision my dad was building, the land he owned, in Kīhei. We stopped going to Maui in the early nineties, but in my youthful arrogance I assumed our trips tapered off because Steve and I had become adults with our own lives. When I cleaned out my dad and Steve's house, I found no record of the Maui project ever existing. No contracts or blueprints, no documentation of a partnership formed or dissolved. Proof of my family's connection to the ʻāina had disappeared, like ephemera streaking across the night sky. Sometimes I entertain a fantasy where I still own the land and get to right my dad's wrong: I sell it to the Native Hawaiian people for $1, and they let me keep a small house on it for no charge. The Hawaiians get their land back, I stay connected to Hawaiʻi and somehow my loss-filled birthright is transmuted into something fertile.

Of course, Matt King's cousins will be less than thrilled about his decision to deprive them of hundreds of millions of dollars. Cousin Hugh warns Matt that they're not intimidated that Matt's a lawyer and will sue his ass. Even before this threat, Beau Bridges plays Hugh, a supposedly laid-back beach bum, with perfectly malevolent undertones. In an earlier scene at Tahiti Nui, Hugh calls his cousin "Matty" and "Matty Boy," sternly reminding him that all The Cousins want to sell to Holitzer (all of them don't). In the book and the original shooting script, Hugh uses Matt's adult name—without that "y" on the end. But Beau Bridges changed it, aware that Hugh is trying to reduce Matt to a child and rob him of his autonomy, much like the original keepers of this land, the Hawaiians, were robbed of theirs.

It's a brilliant interpretation of character, the kind of guy who knows the bartender's first name—and probably just enough about her personal life to ask questions that make him appear thoughtful—and buys other people drinks and is all "Hey, whatever, man" only because someone else is bankrolling his carefree lifestyle. But he's aware that the lifestyle, and the aura it provides him, doesn't belong to him. It belongs to this relative who lives in Hono-fucking-lulu and tucks his aloha shirt into the khaki pants he wears with a belt and believes he's so high and mighty because he actually has an income-producing career.

My brother was like this. Just replace "beach bum" with its mainland synonym: "guy who hangs out at the golf club." Steve received half the profits of my dad's land deals under the guise of working for him. But mostly what Steve did was stay out until three in the morning at bars, sleep until noon, then go to the Cherry Creek Country Club and maybe play a round, but mostly he'd just sit in the bar and buy drinks for his friends. He told women that the house he and my dad lived in was *his* house, and he was letting our dad live there. He told these women our dad actually lived in Canada and just came to visit sometimes. He told women these lies because he knew that a grown man living with and being supported by his father was pathetic. I also think a part of him believed these falsehoods in order for his ego to survive. Every once in a while, my dad appeared to briefly grow a pair and tell Steve that he had to move out. Once he threatened to cut Steve off financially. Steve was so aware that nearly every aspect of his presumed being was based on this illusion, so helpless to what would become of him without it, that he threatened, more than once, to beat up my dad. My dad never made him leave.

Matt and his daughters return to Honolulu to be with Elizabeth. A counselor explains to Scottie that her mother is going to die, while Matt, Alex, and their gray-haired doctor watch with compassion. My attention gets really split at this point in the movie, and an argument could certainly be made that it's because I don't want to be emotionally present in this scene, the one that reminds me of when the doctor told me my comatose mom had no more than twenty-four hours to live. But what I focus on is that the counselor is white. Throughout the entire movie, I've been well aware that brown-skinned locals are only used as background scenery. Yes, this is the story of a haole family—that's inherent in the plot—but why are there so few people of color in their orbit? In Honolulu, white people make up only 23 percent of the population, but the doctor, the counselor, the nurses, all of the Kings' friends, Alex's boyfriend and boarding school RA… they're white. The few *super minor* speaking roles that go to brown-skinned people are: two grade-school teachers, the girl Scottie bullied (she says two words), the girl's mother, the bartender at the Tahiti Nui (who also says two words and doesn't even get a screen credit), Alex's roommate, and one other friend of Scottie's. There's a local band playing Hawaiian music at the Tahiti Nui, and it can be argued that this gives screen time to traditional Hawaiian culture, *or* that it depicts Hawaiians performing for the entertainment of white folks, robbing them of any sovereign dignity. I assure you there are advocates firmly for each camp, and I feel too much of an outsider, too *haole*, to decide which is "right."

I am not, however, too haole to find this whitewashing entirely maddening. It's a persistent Hollywood malady to set movies in Hawai'i for the scenery, for the exoticism, and yet to exclude the people of Hawai'i, as if they have nothing to do with what Hawai'i is. The people are, at best, set decoration. At the worst, locals are played by very white actors, either in brownface (Rob Schneider in *50 First Dates*) or without any pretense at all (Emma Stone as a quarter-Chinese/quarter-Hawaiian character with the last name Ng in *Aloha*). To set a movie in Hawai'i and exclude the people further reinforces the view that their world, their *lives*, are simply products for white main-landers to commodify. It further attempts to divorce them from the 'āina.

In the penultimate scene in *The Descendants*, Matt and his daughters bob in a canoe in the calm waters in front of Waikīkī, preparing to spread Elizabeth's ashes, to return her to the place where she was the most content. Unlike the first scene where Elizabeth speeds further away from Honolulu with each passing second, Matt and his girls simply float in one place. They get no closer, but no further away from the land. The girls take turns gently placing a scoop of their mother's corporeal remains into the ocean, and then Matt dumps in the rest. They place leis—the quintessential symbol of the aloha spirit—in the water to float away with Elizabeth.

I remember riding in the passenger seat while Michael drove us to my dad's funeral, the urn cradled on my lap. This is what becomes of a parent, I thought. My mom's ashes were scattered over Half Moon Bay in California. I'm not entirely sure why, but guess it's because she and my dad traveled there when they were young in their marriage, and she also visited Steve in the Bay Area when he was at San Francisco State University. None were reasons that had anything to do with me. But that's what it was like back then. Steve and my dad were in charge. I was too bereft, they assumed I was too young, to handle the details of death. Seventeen years later, my life was about nothing but the details of death.

In the last scene of *The Descendants*, the camera remains fixed in one place: on the couch in front of the TV, as if the camera and the TV are one and the same. Scottie is curled up underneath the pineapple-colored Hawaiian quilt that had been on her mother's deathbed. She's watching the TV, with Morgan Freeman's familiar voice narrating *March of the Penguins*. Matt comes out of the kitchen with two bowls of ice cream—strawberry for her, mocha chip for him; one a flavor for a child, the other for an adult. He joins Scottie under the quilt as Freeman talks about how isolated Antarctica is, and how, once upon a time, it was tropical. Like Hawai'i.

Alex emerges in the background. She sees her remaining family on the couch, and stands behind them just long enough to let the viewer realize she is making the decision of whether she will be a part of this family, or will contribute more to its fracturing. She sits next to her father on the couch, under the quilt, and Matt hands her his bowl of mocha chip to share. It's creepy, in a way, how Alex shares the grown-up flavor of ice cream with Matt as if they are now a couple. Not that anything incestuous is implied, but this young woman, who has barely had time to figure out who she is, who she wants to be, is elevated to the position of eldest woman in the house. You hear these stories all the time, about the mother who died young and the teen daughter who stood in for her and raised her younger sibling, who had to abandoning her youth for familial responsibilities.

It took a while until I had to fill that role. I was already an adult when Steve and my dad plunged into their mental and physical illnesses, so trying to care for them theoretically didn't cost me my youth. But they spurned all my attempts to help them get better—therapy, addiction treatment, skilled nursing, separation. They were swirling in a Charybdisian maelstrom and wanted to grasp onto me, even if it meant me disappearing into the vortex with them. While Alex could stand behind her father and sister and realize she had the chance to complete something wanting to be whole, my only option for survival was to stand witness as my family was devoured. But, like Alex, it deprived me of whatever remnants of innocence and youth I'd been clinging to.

We know the Kings have money and can afford a housekeeper or nanny or therapist, or whatever else Scottie needs—other than her mother. Matt will spend less time at work, and Alex probably won't go back to boarding school so they can all be together. And because Matt refused to sell the land, they can go to Kaua'i whenever they want. They can feel the sunshine on their skin and the saltwater in their face, and in those moments, they will remember they are alive.

Da Kine | The Big Five

DURING THE PLANTATION ERA THE HAWAIIAN Islands were dominated by "The Big Five" businesses: Castle & Cooke, Alexander & Baldwin, C. Brewer & Co., American Factors (Amfac), and Theo H. Davies & Co. This *may* go without saying, but I'll say it anyway: they were all owned by white guys. The owners were missionaries and the sons of missionaries, American and Welsh businessmen, and a German sea captain. Like all good capitalists, they followed the money trail: their enterprises started in whaling, transitioned to sugar, added pineapple, then transportation and tourism. With that kind of money (and land ownership), the Big Five had tremendous political power that they wanted to keep for themselves, and, more specifically, keep away from Hawaiians. In 1887, some particularly "ambitious" members of the B5 drafted a constitution that stripped King Kalākaua of real power and forced him to sign it at gunpoint, earning the name "The Bayonet Constitution."

Theo Davies, who owned the smallest of the B5, was the black sheep of the group. He spent four years as guardian to Princess Kaʻiulani, heir to the about-to-be-overthrown throne, when she was sent to England to study. After the coup in 1893, Davies accompanied Princess Kaʻiulani to Washington, DC to implore President Cleveland to restore the monarchy (spoiler alert: it didn't work). He was labeled a traitor by his former colleagues. Davies died in 1898, passing the business onto his son. The company

was the first of the B5 to divest from agriculture, selling in 1973 to a Hong Kong conglomerate that later invested in—wait for it—Taco Bell and Pizza Hut. By the early 2000s, THD & Co. had sold all its interests in the Islands.

Amfac filed for bankruptcy in 1998, was bought up and sold off and reorganized, but kept its Kā'anapali assets. In 2017, A&B closed the last sugar mill in the Islands, but don't cry for them: they still own about eighty-seven thousand acres of land. In 1985, Castle & Cooke was bought by David H. Murdock, a billionaire land developer who *Time* magazine once called "an achievement addict." His purchase of C&C included 95 percent ownership of the island of Lāna'i (how's *that* for a value-added perk!). In 2012, Murdock sold Lāna'i to Oracle Corporation cofounder, Larry Ellison. That, of course, is a story all its own....

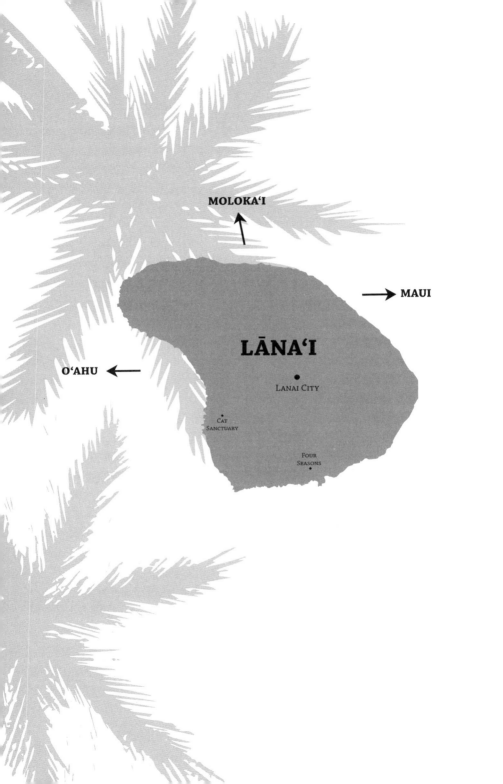

MOLOKA'I

MAUI

LĀNA'I

O'AHU

LANAI CITY

CAT
SANCTUARY

FOUR
SEASONS

ISLAND FOR SALE!

AMAZING OPPORTUNITY TO BUY YOUR OWN ISLAND!

New Listing with Extremely Limited Profit Potential!

Name: Lānaʻi (aka: The Pineapple Isle)
Size: 88,000 acres (98 percent of the island)
Includes: 50 miles of beaches, two resort hotels, two championship golf courses, one country inn, 30 miles of paved roads (no stoplights), a gas station, a grocery store, one-third of all island housing (≈ 500 cottages and luxury homes), horse stables, a skeet shooting range, a central park, a community center, the water company and a waste-water treatment plant, a cemetery, 400 feral cats, and 3,135 people!

Available for Purchase in 2012
Price: $300 million
The Ideal Buyer for This Island Is:
- Worth ≈$46 billion, fluctuating between the 5th–7th richest person in the world;
- The subject of a biography titled *The Difference Between God and Larry Ellison: God Doesn't Think He's Larry Ellison*;
- Owner of a tennis tournament in Indian Wells, CA, an America's Cup sailing team, a $3+ million

car that reaches speeds of 231 mph, an Italian
military jet, 24 Malibu mansions, and approximately 28 percent founding stock in Oracle,
Corp.;
- Willing to embrace a historically unprofitable
property as a "passion purchase";
- Capable of envisioning the island and its residents as "this really cool twenty-first-century
engineering project."

DETAILS

Region: State of Hawai'i, Maui County
Location: Mid-Pacific, just below Tropic of Cancer
Latitude: 20.8166° N
Longitude: 156.9273° W
Topography: Extinct volcano, beaches, pine forests
Method of Sale: "As Is"

Chain of Title
- **Kauluā'au**: A teenager banished to Lāna'i,
which was said to be inhabited by evil man-eating spirits, in the 1500s for the crime of
uprooting breadfruit trees on his native Maui.
When he didn't give up the ghost (due to
man-eating spirits, or starvation and exposure
to the elements), Kauluā'au was rewarded control of Lāna'i, and other Hawaiians settled there.
- **King Kamehameha I**: Decimated the population of Lāna'i in the late 1700s during his

war to conquer and unify the Hawaiian islands, but hey: he got the island! In February 1779, Capt. Charles Clerke was the first European to spot Lāna'i while manning the HMS *Resolution* after Captain Cook's murder on the Big Island eleven days earlier. Unable to spot inhabitants or viable villages (see above, re: Kamehameha), he chose not to land. [Note: it's also possible he was trying to hightail it out of Hawai'i after Cook's murder.]

- **Walter M. Gibson**: Converted to Mormonism the year before arriving on Lāna'i in 1861. Bought a large tract of land (aka: an ahupua'a) from Chief Ha'alelea in 1863 with embezzled funds from the Church of Jesus Christ of Latter Day Saints. Was excommunicated the following year. Over the next 23 years, purchased most of the ahupua'a on Lāna'i. After his death in 1888, title to the land passed to his daughter. The family tried ranching sheep, growing sugarcane, and leasing the land, but none of these ventures were profitable.

- **James Drummond Dole**: Cousin of a missionary who helped draft The Bayonet Constitution, which coincidentally removed Walter M. Gibson (above) as prime minister. Bought Lāna'i for $1.1 million in 1922. Development and improvement projects included: plowing the interior fir forests to plant pineapple fields, erecting a pineapple processing plant, building roads, a boat harbor, and a company town to house his 3,000 mostly Japanese and Filipino laborers.

- **Castle & Cook**e: One of Hawai'i's Big Five companies; took over all of Dole's holdings (incl. Lāna'i) in 1961. Overseas competition drove down the price of pineapple, and Castle & Cooke teetered on bankruptcy.
- **David H. Murdock**: California billionaire, bought Castle & Cooke in 1985 (including Lāna'i). Shifted Lāna'i's economy to tourism, building two resorts run by Four Seasons. The residents, who he referred to as "his children," were allowed to transition from agrarian labor to hotel jobs. Murdock ultimately viewed the island as a money pit, ceased upkeep of the infrastructure, and laid off numerous workers. He referred to Lāna'i as "the poorest financial investment I've made in my entire life."

Are You the Next Owner of Lāna'i?

YOU will prove to be smarter, more innovative, and more caring than the previous owner(s). YOU will make this island *work*. Your mandate will be ***compassionate luxury*** ("more than just a phrase, it's an action of purpose"). Creating a utopia on Lāna'i may require shuttering both resorts for multimillion-dollar renovations. Your compassion will steer you to retain all 650 hotel employees in other jobs (without tips, this may cut their incomes by 50%, but you know it's only temporary!). Income for other island businesses—restaurants, hair salons, art galleries, etc.—will decline 50–60% without tourism, but, again, it's only temporary! (Temporary = a minimum of 1 year, a maximum of ???). Local entrepreneurs may approach your Hawaiian-named management company for business leases—or even to propose partnerships—but you'll offer them jobs instead, because you know they'll be better off working for *you*.

YOU will be the landlord and employer of the majority of the island's residents, and YOU will have the power to enrich the residents' lives. You will spruce up neglected buildings, prune local flora, restore the movie theater, launch a kids' summer program, bankroll free Pilates and water aerobics classes and 'ukulele lessons, pay for residents to get their cats dewormed (oh, all those cats!), open a domestic violence shelter for women, install 4G cellular service, and reopen the community pool (closed by the previous owner to cut costs. But YOU don't care about profit. You are in it for the *experiment*)!

You also have the ability to remain INVISIBLE to the people of Lānaʻi. You can form a management company (with an Hawaiian name, natch) and appoint a Lānaʻi-born COO to be your proxy-on-the-ground. That's not to say you'll never visit the island; locals will know when you're around because they'll see your 288-foot yacht hitched in the harbor. Residents may wish you'd attend a town meeting, but you know chaos would ensue if a person of YOUR STATURE showed up at their cozy ILWU Hall.

YOU will rescue Lānaʻi from its meek roots of fishing and sustenance farming and failed pineapple picking to make it ***the premier luxury destination*** in Hawai'i. The newly renovated Four Seasons Resort(s)' room product will offer an *authentic* Hawaiian experience, starting at $1,300 per night. Shops will carry Diane von Furstenberg dresses and Jimmy Choo shoes. Guests can eat at Nobu (owned by Robert Di Niro!), Malibu Farm, or One Forty, serving Catalan shrimp, Alaskan king crab, and steaks from Idaho. Although none of these luxury amenities will be affordable for island residents, they *will* benefit from a wealthier caliber of tourist dropping money into the local economy. The island's one art gallery will report selling an unprecedented number of paintings of palm trees, surfboards, and plumeria.

You must be prepared for *some* setbacks. ☹ For example, if the Lāna'i Planning Commission approves a 15-year permit for your proposed desalination plant, instead of the 30 years *you want*, you can refuse to build it. Clearly, those people don't understand the stakes! Don't they realize their island has scant usable water, and without YOUR desalination plant, economic development will be greatly curbed? But as a (successful!) businessman, you know working with a 15-year permit wouldn't be a good *investment*. You also know there is no such thing as failure, only opportunity. Maybe your $15 million hydroponic greenhouse will work out better?!

Some media and residents will refer to you as the island's SAVIOR; others will be reflexively skeptical, noting that since Walter M. Gibson (see above, re: Chain of Title), Lāna'i "has been owned and exploited by one really rich guy or another." A Catholic priest will lead his congregation in asking God to bless you! Some citizens will say that others welcome your improvements and infusion of cash only because they "don't know any other way to live but under some sort of feudal-serf system." One man will tell the *NYT* that while the money sounds great now, what happens if, in five years, you don't want to play this game anymore? What if you get bored of this *experiment*? Then the people of Lānaʻi will be SOL. But just because you are often quoted as saying, "Five years from now, I don't know how I'll think" about *other* business ventures doesn't mean that's what will happen here. Five years from now you might still be jazzed about converting island agriculture to mass hydroponics! Rest easy: to control unfair characterizations about you, you can insist all your employees sign **Do Not Disclose** agreements, and the unilateral power **YOU** wield will intimidate the remaining island residents into speaking cautiously, if at all.

*If **YOU** are ready to dive into this new adventure, this **lab experiment**, this opportunity to restore the Aloha Spirit to Lānaʻi, contact an agent today at Islandsforsale.com!*

Da Kine | The Forbidden Isle

Nɪʻɪʜᴀᴜ, Hᴀᴡᴀɪʻɪ's ᴏᴛʜᴇʀ ᴘʀɪᴠᴀᴛᴇʟʏ ᴏᴡɴᴇᴅ ɪsʟᴀɴᴅ, couldn't have less in common with Lānaʻi. It's been owned by the same family since 1850, when New Zealander Elizabeth Sinclair purchased it for $10,000 in gold. In 1915 her descendant, Aubrey Robinson, closed the island to outsiders, maintaining it as a homeland for Native Hawaiians. To this day there are no hotels, stores, gas stations, paved roads, or indoor plumbing. School is taught in ʻōlelo Hawaiʻi. Until recently, no one could even step foot on the island unless expressly invited by a Niʻihau resident or the Robinson family, earning its moniker "The Forbidden Island."

In 1984, six hundred Hawaiians lived on Niʻihau. Today, there are about 170, and only half are full-time residents. What caused this great population decline? Lack of employment, for one. Residents once worked on the Robinson's cattle ranch, harvested kiawe, or kept bees. By 1999 all these ventures shuttered, and the islanders were plunged into unemployment. Their only source of income became intricate leis crafted of tiny Niʻihau shells. But one lei takes a year to make and sells for $1,000 to $10,000, so they're not exactly the most reliable revenue stream. Niʻihauans left to get jobs, and to pursue higher education, and because humans always wonder what else is out there.

Now the Robinsons run helicopter tours to Niʻihau. For $440, a tourist can snorkel on a secluded beach for a half day. If that's too tame, then a $1,950/person safari allows them to hunt wild boar and hybrid sheep (+ $1,300 per "hunting spouse"). But no matter how much you pay, whether you're there to swim or to shoot, tourists are still kept away from the village and its residents. The owners want to keep the islanders safe from tourism for as long as they can.

Pass the Tabu: Here's the Story of the Brady Bunch in Hawai'i

Aᴤᴋ ᴀ ᴍᴇᴍʙᴇʀ ᴏꜰ Gᴇɴᴇʀᴀᴛɪᴏɴ X ᴡʜᴇʀᴇ ᴛʜᴇʏ ɢᴏᴛ
their original ideas about Hawai'i, and they'll inevitably mention *Hawaii Five-O* or *The Brady Bunch*. The
former was inarguably the cooler of the two, with its
thrilling intro of exotic Honolulu sights set to the surf
song-meets-tribal beat theme. But since I'm basically
uncool, the first images of Hawai'i that have stuck with
me all these years originated from *The Brady Bunch*.

"Hawaii Bound," the first of three episodes in which
the Brady family visits Honolulu, premiered on ABC
on September 22, 1972. It was an era when the mount-
ing death toll in Vietnam, widespread riots and protests,
police brutality, and the unfolding Watergate scandal
constantly hovered in the American psyche, render-
ing us unable to recover from the moral hangover the
sixties had wrought. Television was already working to
distract us from the news of the day ("Hey, I know you
just saw Walter Cronkite reporting on some disturbing
shit, but stay tuned to see what antics Gilligan gets himself into this week!"), and in the fall of 1969, *The Brady*

Bunch claimed its place in the pharmacopeia of televised narcotics. The main difference between *The Brady Bunch* and escape-from-realty sitcoms like *I Dream of Jeannie* and *The Beverly Hillbillies* is that, somehow, Brady creator Sherwood Schwartz actually thought he was making a socially relevant show.

Schwartz and his son, Lloyd, wrote a terrible book called *Brady, Brady, Brady: The Complete Story of The Brady Bunch as Told by the Father/Son Team Who Really Know*. In this painful slog, Schwartz said his intention was to depict the complicated reality of modern blended families. Of course, he didn't even come close to doing so, skirting such relevant issues as the boys' grief over their mother's death, the girls' anger about their totally absent father (who/where the hell *was* that guy?), and the kids' resentment about being expected to just move on and instantly call these virtual strangers Mom and Daddy. Beyond potential difficulties relating to their immediate living situation, the blended bunch also never had money problems, serious health issues, drug addictions, unplanned pregnancies, sexual assault, or most certainly: death. There was no conundrum that couldn't be solved in one episode with a dose of family love, dumb jokes, and—eek—wisdom.

When I re-watched the *Brady Bunch* episodes set in Hawai'i, I didn't expect them to, in any way, reflect reality in the Islands. I was ready to call out every single way the producers had misrepresented Hawaiian culture. Yes, the second and third episodes of the arc are especially silly and take plenty of liberties with reality, but the first episode rang surprisingly true—or, at least, true to the touristic experience of Hawai'i. And the touristic experience of Hawai'i isn't completely accurate or inaccurate, but represents the surface of a much deeper, darker, and more nuanced story. The real Hawai'i lies just beneath, if you're willing to dig.

In Which the Brady Kids Break Their Parents' Eardrums by Repeatedly Shrieking, "We're Going to Hawai'i!"

"Hawaii Bound" begins when Mike, the Brady patriarch, arrives home with a mysterious ribbon-wrapped box. Lovely Lady Carol and the six kids torture viewers with a painful amount of "What is it? What is it?" from the moment the box is presented, to when Carol removes the green ribbon and takes off the box top, to when she sees there are plane tickets inside, to when—after a minute and forty-two seconds of this—Mike *finally* reveals that the brood is going to Hawai'i. The announcement causes the kids to erupt into a frenzy so loud and energetic you'd think they'd just been promised a trip to the moon. Although, in all fairness, for most of the twentieth century Hawai'i had been advertised as just that exotic, so maybe their reaction had some basis in reality. [Note: you'll often notice me attempting to compare the Brady Bunch with *reality*, which I realize seems somewhat ridiculous. Bear with me.]

Tourism to Hawai'i had been steadily increasing since statehood in 1959, and experienced a boom in the early seventies. Travel historians (yes, there is such a thing) often claim it's because tickets from the West Coast started being offered for "only" $100. However, when accounting for inflation, that's about $588 in today's money, which is not what you'd call affordable for an average family of four. Of course, the Bradys aren't a family of four, but eight—nine, when you add in housekeeper Alice—bringing the cost to fly the clan to Hawai'i in at over $5,000 (today's value). But Mike didn't have to pay that price tag, or for the three rooms at the brand-new Sheraton Waikiki (as usual, it's unclear where Alice sleeps). Mike's boss, Mr. Phillips, sent him and the family to Honolulu so Mike could "check in on" the construction of a building he designed. Now *that's* a nice boss. In an exterior shot of a United Airlines DC-8 flying over the ocean, there's a voiceover conversation in which Carol tells Mike that she's going to send Mr. Phillips a thank-you postcard every single day.

"This is a *business* trip," Mike reminds her.

I'm not sure if that means they aren't supposed to have fun—in which case, don't bring the entire family and the housekeeper along—or if it's a reminder that Mike couldn't afford this extravaganza on his own. In many other ways, this episode reads as a marketing campaign from the Hawai'i Visitors and Convention Bureau, and you'd think they'd *want* viewers to believe a Hawaiian vacation is affordable for the typical American family. But this one line signals that the Bradys aren't rich or high-falutin, and are therefore likeable—which means viewers will want what they have.

In Which Girls in Bikinis (and Coconut Bras) Are Just Part of the Scenery

When the Bradys descend the open-air staircase at Honolulu International Airport, two thin, scantily clad brown-skinned women place leis around their necks and kiss their cheeks. Although the lei greeting, as common arrival procedure, was starting to be phased out in 1972, it was—and remains—a significant iconography of visiting the Islands. It also allows the first opportunity for oldest son Greg to ogle the local women. He even tries to pull the lei greeter in for a make-out session. Mike yanks him back, saving the woman from what we would now call sexual harassment by a creep, but in Bradyville it was a funny "boys will be boys" bit.

Hawai'i's women (especially the thin, bikini-clad ones) began to be commoditized in the early twentieth century as part of the exotic/erotic fantasy of the Islands. Since then, they have been plastered on postcards and calendars and drink coasters and drink cozies to provide entertainment and arousal for white men. This is especially true in the case of hula dancer, whose swinging hips and flat, bare stomach are as much a symbol of tourist Hawai'i as the pineapple or orchid lei. The poignant difference between these women, and pineapples and leis, is that the latter are agricultural products and hula dancers are human beings. But they are equally commoditized in the marketing of a Polynesian paradise.

"The Girls," as the Brady females are called, take a hula lesson on the lawn of their Waikīkī hotel. Their instructor is played by a former Miss Kaua'i named Elithe Aguiar, who was also the sarong-wearing woman running down the beach in the *Hawaii Five-O* opening. Aguiar never speaks in her *Brady Bunch* appearance. She dances, and The Girls try to imitate their mute teacher with comic incompetence. Alice throws out her back and is in so much pain she can't even move, but Aguiar just watches— never says a word, never moves to help, as if she's incapable of doing anything but pleasantly swinging her hips and waving her arms. She never even tells the women what the dance, what the moves they are making, mean.

The meaning of hula dances a crooked path, and Hawaiian historians can't seem to agree on its origins and purpose. Some say that it was initially danced by goddesses, and some say it was first danced *for* goddesses. Some say it was primarily a religious act, while others contend the hula was mainly for entertainment. Some assert that originally only men danced hula, while others point out there's zero evidence to support that, and *some* evidence proving it was always a coed endeavor. Scholars can't even agree on whether the white missionaries who came to the Islands in the 1820s actually banned the hula. It's a widely reported factoid, but many historians contend that while the missionaries disapproved of hula (calling it a "heathen dance"), they didn't have the authority to ban it. As a result, it receded and was publicly practiced less often, but it's not clear that there was an actual law against it.

What historians and scholars do agree on is that tourism radically transformed hula. Ancient Hawaiians considered hula sacred, even when practiced as entertainment. It connected the body and the heart with the earthly elements. When it was seized as entertainment for white visitors, the sacred aspect was jettisoned. Intricately woven costumes gave way to grass skirts and coconut shell bras. Chanting and poetry was replaced by 'ukuleles. The hula was both sexualized and diminished into a novelty act performed between tourists turning up their noses at poi and digging into kālua pig.

Greg Brady's objectification of the women of Hawai'i becomes an actual theme of "Hawaii Bound." After David, a construction worker-turned-island tour guide, shows the family local sights, Greg asks him when they can see the "real sights"—girls in bikinis! Actually, he doesn't even say "girls in." He just says "bikinis," as if the bikinis are walking around independent of a human being, just another object for Greg's gratification. We even get to see him in action: he lies on the beach watching women walk by, the camera mostly trained to expose their bodies, but not their faces. When Greg finally decides to make a move on a Bikini, it's not a local woman; it's a blonde, blue-eyed Californian named Mandy, teleported straight from a Beach Boys song. You can ogle the brown-skinned women, is the message, but for a white boy to talk to one? That was tabu.

In Which Wise Brown-Skinned Folks Enlighten White People About Native Myths

The first time the viewer hears the word "tabu," the Bradys are returning from the USS *Arizona* Memorial. David says there's an old story about Pearl Harbor that most people don't know. When construction began on the port, an "old island chief" (an ali'i) warned them it was tabu. The bay was the home of the shark queen and, if they built on it, evil things would happen. Sure enough, when the Navy was constructing the first dry dock, it collapsed into the sea. "No one knew why," David says. "And after that, nothing bad happened again…until the attack of 1941."

Mike jumps in with, "Well, I hardly think that has anything to do with the tabu, kids."

"Well, neither do I, Mr. Brady," David says. "But, you know, some of these old islanders are pretty superstitious."

A couple of things here: It's true that Native Hawaiians believed the Queen Shark god Ka'ahupahau lived in the coral caves under Pearl Harbor and protected them. And it's true that Native Hawaiians were vocally opposed to the development of Pearl Harbor—not just because it might upset Ka'ahupahau, but because the bay was a sacred site. The part where David's story gets a little spongy is this idea that an island chief/ali'i warned them against it, and that these old islanders are simply superstitious.

Construction on the dock began in 1909, but the system in which ali'i held a position of prominence and respect (or any position at all, for that matter) had disappeared around fifteen years earlier when the United States overthrew the Hawaiian monarchy. Even before then, the number of ali'i had diminished greatly under Kamehameha I's rule, and as Western influence shaped Hawaiian governance. In all the accounts I've read about the brouhaha over building Pearl Harbor, the concerns were never ascribed to one specific person, one chief, one "superstitious old islander." Instead, the outcry is attributed to Native Hawaiians as a group. This difference is not insignificant. Ascribing the concern, as David does, to one old guy whose place in society was phased out decades ago reduces him to an anomaly, a kook, even. But if it had been rightly attributed to the long-held beliefs of Hawaiians en masse, it would bring their outrage over the United States bulldozing their culture to the forefront. And I bet that's a can of worms no one wanted to open to tourists in 1972.

So, yes, the Hawaiian people did vocally oppose the construction and the US military charged ahead anyway, and yes, the first dry dock sunk in 1913. To say that no one had any idea *why* is inaccurate, since engineers declared it was due to underground pressure and seismic disturbances. This seems pretty plausible, considering the entire Hawaiian archipelago is a web of volcanoes born of violent plate tectonics. Many Hawaiians did believe the dock accident was the wrath of Ka'ahupahau, which I'm not entirely willing to discount, either. The US took a two-pronged approach to rectifying the issue—neither of which involved *not* constructing a naval base on sacred land. First, they devised a new building plan that accounted for the geology of the bay, and second, they brought in a kahuna (a Hawaiian priest/healer/shaman) to bless the location. This winning combination kept the new dry dock from capsizing.

From the deft storytelling hand of the Schwartz team, we know this legend about ignoring tabu serves as a foreshadowing of future events for the family. This unfurls in the very next scene at the construction site for the building Mike is checking on. One aspect of this scene that's unexpectedly cool is that all the construction workers are local, meaning brown-skinned. This may seem like, "Well, sure—who else would be playing these parts?" except that films and TV shows set in Hawai'i have the maddening habit of casting mostly white people in speaking roles, even though Caucasians only account for about 27 percent of the state's population.

The younger of the two local workers uncovers the idol that drives the plot for the three-episode arc. It's a small, rectangular tiki—a representation of an ancient god—carved into weathered white wood or stone. The young guy moves to pick it up, but is warned by Old Mr. Hanalei to leave it alone. "No, *tabu*," Hanalei says. "Tabu very strong. Bring evil to all who touch."

"Oh, come on, Bruddha," the younger guy says. "That's just an old island superstition."

Kapu, a complex system of social hierarchy and forbidden actions, governed ancient Hawai'i. Kapu behaviors—that is, tabu ones—ranged from walking or standing in the shadow of an ali'i, men and women eating together, and for women to consume pork or bananas. Punishment for breaking kapu could be banishment to a penal colony, or even execution.

The Brady Bunch's interchangeability of the words "kapu" and "tabu" has a legitimate basis, by the way: when the Hawaiian alphabet was developed by white missionaries in the early 1820s, it initially included a t and a b. A few years later, they eliminated both because they were considered phonetically redundant to the k and the p. But the t and b still existed in documents written during those in-between years, accounting for how the words tabu and kapu are sometimes used synonymously.

The kapu system was a sacred legal and social institution, and it would be considered pretty darn disrespectful for modern Hawaiians to refer to it as "superstition." I give that inaccuracy a pass here, because 1) it's *The Brady Bunch*; and 2) it was a sign of the times that young people were wary of the older generation's ideas and institutions. This is further reinforced when the younger worker carelessly tosses the idol aside to appease Hanalei.

"Someday you learn respect," Hanalei tells him. "Respect for island tabu."

The warning has a "pay attention to your elders"/"those who ignore the past are doomed to repeat it" vibe that's relevant in almost any generation, but especially in 1972, when young people were saying, "Fuck that and fuck you" to their elders—to their *grand* elder, the government.

Later that day (or maybe the next? Time is fluid in Bradyville and on Hawaiian holiday), Mike takes the boys to the construction site. While mucking around without supervision or hardhats, Bobby discovers the tiki idol. After he and Peter joke about how ugly it is—a great way to appease the gods, by the way—Bobby declares it his good luck charm. Conveniently, this ancient Hawaiian artifact already has a hole drilled through the top, so Bobby puts it on a string to wear around his neck.

That night, the boys are going to bed early, without their parents telling them to. Greg wants to rest up since he'll be in a surfing contest the next day. Never mind that Greg is eighteen, an age at which it seems perfectly reasonable to stay up all night drinking and smoking weed, even if you have an important event the next morning (like, for instance, taking the SATs. Not that I have any personal experience doing that). Bobby and Peter are needling Greg that he's going to get creamed in the competition, since Hawaiians can practically surf before they can walk. Greg tells them there are great surfers all over the world, and his brothers remind him he's not one of them. Greg throws a pillow in their direction, but it hits the wall, instead (showcasing his exceptional athletic abilities). A large metal sculpture—a giant leaf, I think—falls off the wall and almost brains Bobby. He manages to move out of the way and credits his good luck charm, the tiki idol, with saving his life.

In Which the Author Experiences Major Heebie-Jeebies

When I mentioned to friends that I was rewatching the Hawai'i episodes of *The Brady Bunch*, several gleefully shouted, "The tarantula!" This is because a couple nights after the sculpture almost kills Bobby, Peter wears the tiki idol to bed and awakens to a big, brown, hairy spider staring him down. Greg knocks the spider off Peter's chest with a shoe, and the boys hop up the bed and do the heebie-jeebie dance. Mike comes in to tell them to keep down the racket, so they point out the spider on the floor. He informs them there's nothing to worry about, because there are no poisonous spiders in Hawai'i. What a convenient morsel of trivia for Mike to know! It's one of those moments I feel certain that muckety-mucks from the Hawai'i Visitors Bureau were, at the very least, giving notes on the script:

- *If tourists think we have dangerous spiders, they may not come*

- *Make sure people know we only have friendly spiders here—you know, spiders with the Aloha Spirit!*

My response to even *thinking* about spiders is similar to the boys' high-pitched freak out, and I took no pleasure in the approximately fifteen minutes I spent researching whether they actually used a tarantula or a local arachnid—like the incredibly creepy cane spider—in the scene. Ultimately, it was Schwartz's book that confirmed the arachnid in question really was a tarantula, requiring a "spider wrangler" on set to place little plastic caps on its fangs.

Another piece of propaganda widely spread about Hawai'i is that there are no snakes. This is mostly true. Terrestrial snakes are not endemic to Hawai'i, and somehow didn't hitch a ride with any of the folks who settled or colonized the archipelago. It's illegal to bring a snake into Hawai'i or even to own one, punishable by a $200,000 fine and up to three years in jail. Snakes feed on bird eggs, and introducing them to the fragile ecosystem of Hawai'i could easily decimate its exotic bird population. The mongoose provides an excellent cautionary tale (how often do you get to say *that* phrase?) of how things can go down. Plantation owners brought the mongoose to Hawai'i in the 1800s to eradicate rats, but it turned out mongoose also ate bird eggs and they nearly destroyed the now-endangered nēnē goose population (while having no effect on the rat population, since rats are nocturnal, and mongoose aren't).

Nonetheless, idiots continue to smuggle snakes into the state. Local news is sprinkled with stories of an innocent bystander running into a ball python on a Maui coffee farm, for instance, or a boa constrictor on the Pali Highway. (One driver told a Honolulu newspaper that he'd exclaimed, "*Yo, that's a snake!*" when he ran over a boa constrictor, but his friends told him, "*You're tripping!*"). Experts agree, however, that snakes and spiders don't pose a big threat for visitors. The real danger lies in the ocean.

In Which Greg Nearly Drowns in Perhaps the Saddest Wipeout in Surfing History

Back when Greg asked David when he could see bikinis, David mentioned he was judging a surfing contest the next day and Greg should come watch. Greg let David know that he's done some surfing, and would it be okay if he joined the contest? And David was all, "No problem!"

In real life, that actually might be a problem. First of all, most surfing competitions in Hawai'i are invitationals. Secondly, outside haoles aren't easily welcomed into the surfing ranks. Locals harbor resentment about them coming in *again* and trying to appropriate something that was invented by and has cultural significance to Hawaiians.

In ancient times, Hawaiians didn't only surf for fun in between spearfishing and hut construction; he'e nalu (translation: "wave sliding") was an integral part of society. Ali'i used the strength and skill required to affirm their dominance. The kapu system determined that premium wood, like the wiliwili or koa tree, was saved for making surfboards for the ruling class. Commoners' boards were often constructed from something as clunky as a banana tree trunk. Ali'i would even save the good surfing beaches for themselves, designating them kapu to anyone else.

When Captain Cook first arrived in Kaua'i in 1778, surfing was at its peak, and his crew sketched pictures of the natives riding waves. Many of the sailors couldn't even swim and were impressed with the strength and chutzpah the sport required. Sadly, the white missionaries who swept in forty years later weren't nearly as impressed. As they spread the ideals of Christianity in their attempts to tame the heathens, they pressured Hawaiians to wear more clothing, work harder, and play less. This Puritan moral code didn't leave much room for surfing, and the sport nearly died out by the late 1880s.

Interest was renewed in the early 1900s when Jack London and a mainlander named Alexander Hume Ford came to the Islands, and a half-Hawaiian surfer named George Freeth went to California. All three parties obsessively promoted the sport, and—since it's pretty fucking cool—international passion for surfing caught on fast. The resurgence resulted in the formation of the Outrigger Canoe Club on Waikīkī Beach, which was devoted to the preservation of Native Hawaiian Sports. Ironically, but perhaps not surprisingly, for several years (decades?) after WWII, the Outrigger Canoe Club was a haole-only organization. Regarding the membership policies of those years, the 2008 club president said, "The club was not any more prejudiced than other organizations at that time. It wasn't right, but it was the times." What's Hawaiian for *Oy*?

Right after the Outrigger Club was founded, surfing's baton got handed off to Duke Kahanamoku, a Hawaiian Olympic swimmer who gave surfing demonstrations on his international travels. Handsome and elegant, Duke exemplified the dignity of the sport and became an unofficial worldwide ambassador for Hawai'i. Even today, surfing remains one of the last vestiges of Native Hawaiian culture that is prized in *and* out of the Islands.

Since white folks have a pretty bad track record with coming in and a) destroying Hawaiian culture, or b) appropriating and belittling it, Hawaiians don't always welcome them on the waves. An extreme example occurred in 1975, when white Australians were winning the big wave competitions on O'ahu and thumping their chests about being superior to the Hawaiians. Hawaiian surfers were so pissed that they not only kicked the shit out of the Australians, they put a *contract* out on their lives. Eddie Aikau, a legendary North Shore surfer, stepped in and arranged a sit-down with the two biggest offenders, Wayne "Rabbit" Bartholomew and Iain Cairns. Bartholomew described it as a trial where he and Cairns needed to defend themselves in front of a tribunal. Aikau explained how much white outsiders have taken from the Hawaiian people and how infuriating it was that Bartholomew and Cairns were trying to steal one of the last great artifacts of their culture. The Aussies apparently showed adequate contrition, and were allowed not only to live, but also to continue surfing big wave competitions.

Not that Greg Brady would brag excessively about his own skills, though, since those Bradys are such nice kids with good manners. Plus, Greg isn't really much of a surfer. In *Growing Up Brady*, Barry Williams admits that he oversold his surfing ability to the producers, not just so he could perform his own stunts, but so they'd pay for an extra week in Hawai'i prior to filming so he could get used to the waves. This ploy earned him respect from my teenage psyche, which is something I never thought I'd say about anyone on that show.

At the beginning of Greg's Big Surfing Adventure, the other competitors—all either naturally brown-skinned or deeply tanned—paddle out ahead of Greg because he stops *again* to ask David when they'll go look at bikinis. David tells him to maybe stop thinking about that shit and keep his eyes on the waves.

What ultimately happens to Greg is legendary in Bradyworld. As he takes his second heat, Peter and Bobby note from the beach, "Wow, that sure is a big wave!" It's actually not even close to a big wave, somewhere in the 3- to 5-foot range, depending on who you ask. Waves are measured differently in Hawai'i than everywhere else. Most surf cultures measure the height of the wave from the front—that is, from the crest to the surface of the ocean. (This may seem obvious, but it's not like someone's pulling out a measuring tape while in the barrel of a wave; these measurements are more like educated guesses.) When I was a teen, my local pals told me that Hawai'i waves are measured from the back of the wave, and this number is *half* of the front. So what would be called a twelve-foot wave in California would be a six-foot wave in Hawai'i. You only have to look at a wave from the side to realize this isn't accurate. The back is more like two-thirds the height of the front.

One theory proposes that the whole "double the measurement to get the true size of the wave" idea was invented to deter dumbass mainlanders like Greg from biting off more than they can chew. If a mainlander hears a local say, "The waves are eight feet today," then they'll think, "Oh, that actually means *sixteen* feet, which is too much for me!" I offer this theory not as fact or proof of anything, other than the locals' desire to keep certain people out of the water.

The "wow that sure is a big wave" wave that Greg rides is about chest high. Williams calls it five feet in his book. Based on visual evidence, I assume that's by California measurement, but either way, it's relatively small. Greg wipes out, disappears underwater, and then doesn't come back up. The family freaks out! Where's Greg? His board popped up, but he didn't. Did he drown? Is he dead? Wait, there he is, flailing in completely calm waters and gasping for air. Oh my God, Dad better run in and save him!

I'm guessing I wasn't the only viewer who found this wipeout really lame, because in the Schwartz's book they say—basically unprompted—that while the wave Greg wiped out on looked small, the conditions were actually quite dangerous because rocks and coral reefs lurked just under the surface. Well, *duh*. This is a chain of volcanic islands. Reefs are part of what makes classic surfing waves break in the first place. Even Captain Cook's crew recorded this danger in their journals of 1778. Either way, the Brady kids suspect the real reason Greg almost drowned is because he was wearing the tiki idol. Maybe it isn't good luck after all, they conclude. Maybe it's tabu!

In Which the Astute Viewer Realizes Casualties and Guided Missiles Aren't Usually Part of *The Brady Bunch*

On their tour on Honolulu, David proudly narrates that 'Iolani Palace is "the only royal palace in the United States." The building is an amazing anomaly, especially since it's downtown amid high-rise buildings, with a Starbucks and a YMCA a block away. When my husband and I were driving around trying to find it, I looked up from my iPhone and said, "It should be around here. Look for something that looks like a palace." It's not something you say every day in the US. And sure enough, I glanced to my left and there was a thirty-seven-thousand-square-foot American Florentine-style edifice with ornate towers on each corner, two even taller towers in the middle, Corinthian columns lining massive lanais, a coronation pavilion, and a wrought-iron gate adorned with a royal crest.

What David doesn't mention to the Bradys is that when a United States-backed group overthrew the monarchy in 1893, it commandeered the palace and renamed it the "Executive Building." The self-appointed government imprisoned Queen Lili'uokalani in a palace bedroom for participating in the rebellion against the folks who had deposed her (how dare she!). The US supplanters sold, auctioned off, or just downright stole many of the palace's most treasured belongings. Modern-day curators at 'Iolani Palace are managing to track down and restore some of the pilfered artifacts, but many are forever gone.

The Brady crew next views the statue of Kamehameha the Great, where David explains that he was "the first island chief to get all the islands under one rule, so he was our first king." The line feels lifted straight out of a tourist guide and a certain kind of history book, crediting Kamehameha with unifying the eight islands, all of which were engaged in civil wars. But it's not as if Kamehameha was some great diplomat, sailing from island to island to meet with all the ali'i and brokering a unifying peace accord. What he actually did was wage two decades of bloody war.

Kamehameha started his campaign in 1782 by conquering his home territory of the Big Island. Two haole war advisors helped him amass an arsenal of guns and cannons, and he mobilized an armada to invade the neighbor islands. Especially bloody battles were fought on Maui and O'ahu, decimating the populations and landscapes. By the end of the eighteenth century, Kamehameha had established rule over all the islands except Kaua'i. The main reason he hadn't yet claimed Kaua'i isn't because its warriors were exceedingly fierce—although their battle skills weren't negligible, either—but mostly due to the island's lack of proximity. Seventy-two miles from O'ahu, Kaua'i wasn't super accessible, especially in the notoriously strong currents of the Ka'ie'ie Waho channel. Kamehameha's men had to abandon their attack on Kaua'i due to high winds and capsizing canoes on at least one occasion. Nonetheless, Kaua'i's highest ali'i saw the writing on the wall and ceded his island in order to avoid massive bloodshed. The Kingdom of Hawai'i was officially formed in 1810 with Kamehameha as its first king, and the civil wars eradicated. So, while Hawaiians say that Kamehameha unified the Hawaiian Islands, they could just as easily claim he conquered them.

War, as a concept, is almost entirely absent in *The Brady Bunch*. The series aired concurrent with the Vietnam War, and yet was never of concern to the Bradys. Greg never got called to duty, nor did his friends, and Marcia avoided mourning a boyfriend who was shipped out and killed or returned ravaged by war. This glaring lack of war makes it all the more surprising when it sneaks into "Hawaii Bound." David orates that Pearl Harbor is the largest naval installation in the Pacific, while the family "ooohs" and "ahhhs" over nuclear submarines and destroyers armed with guided missiles. The site of these intimidating masses of steel loaded with weapons is already incongruent enough with the whole *Brady Bunch* vibe, but the stakes are raised as the brood continues to the USS *Arizona* Memorial.

Mike-the-Architect points out that the design of the gently sloping monument, lower in the middle and higher on the ends, is symbolic of "the ultimate victory"—presumably, the US dropping an atomic bomb on Hiroshima. The family contemplates the doomed ship and the 1,117 men resting beneath them, while Mike reads part of the plaque aloud:

Dedicated to the eternal memory of our gallant shipmates in the USS Arizona who gave their lives on 7 December, 1941. From today on the USS Arizona will again fly our country's flag just as proudly as she did on the morning of 7 December, 1941.

It's a totally weird WTF moment, so completely out of sync with the show's usual mood, where nothing is serious and no one is mortal. For the whole episode, the Bradys lifted their activities straight from a tourism guidebook: visiting the Hanaloa blowhole, paddling an outrigger canoe off Waikīkī beach, taking in the view of Honolulu from Puʻu ʻUalakaʻa point and giggling at their mangled attempts to pronounce the name. It's possible the producers thought it would be unrealistic to omit Honolulu's number one tourist attraction simply because it's too morbid, but again, *The Brady Bunch* isn't predicated on realism. What this feels like it serves as, instead, is pro-military/pro-war propaganda in a benign package. Not only does this segment highlight the US military as a force to be reckoned with, but also reinforces the idea that to die in battle is an honor. What a relief that must have been to the thousands of people protesting the Vietnam war, being arrested and maced and even shot, to readers of the Pentagon Papers who were learning how the US government engineered the conflict in Vietnam to serve its own purposes, to the loved ones of the tens of thousands of young men who were killed, to the men who returned home more incomplete in their body, mind, and soul than before they left.

"Pearl Harbor sure is impressive," Carol says as they leave the scene.

In Which We Contemplate the Way They All Became the Brady Bunch in Hawaiʻi

Loss is the story of Hawaiʻi—loss of culture, sovereignty, dignity, and life—and it all lingers just below the surface of the Brady excursion. I'm sure it wasn't expected that anyone would dig deeper, not in 1972, and certainly not forty-four years after its original airing. America was supposed to take the representations at face value. But again and again I found myself wondering: how did this episode come about? Between the on-point touristic message and the pro-war propaganda, it feels like the story had some profound intention. However, I've found no proof of that. I kept thinking I'd finally unearth that one interview, that one article, that one document explaining how the Hawai'i Visitors Bureau contacted ABC or Paramount Studios, or vice versa, with a win-win proposition: set a three-episode arc in Hawai'i, which will guarantee high ratings for the show and a boost in tourism for the state. And if Americans end up feeling more secure about their military's actions? Well, that's a bonus.

But I'm also not convinced that the lack of proof means those messages were all an accident. As hard a time as I've given him, Sherwood Schwartz wasn't mindless. For instance, he didn't envision *Gilligan's Island* as just some goofball comedy. He considered the show a "social microcosm" and a philosophical metaphor for all the nations of the world having to work together toward the common goal of global survival. While Schwartz may not have realized his original vision of *The Brady Bunch* being socially relevant, the Hawai'i episodes exposed the ailments of modern society: sexism, racism, materialism, war, and Americans' desperate desire to escape—whether it be into the ordinary television, or to an exotic, Polynesian, middle-class dream.

Da Kine | Aloha Spirit

The Hawai'i Constitution (Revised Statutes 5-7.5) dictates that government officials behave with the "Aloha Spirit": kindness, harmony, pleasantness, modesty, and patience. They even acronymized ALOHA, with each letter representing a Hawaiian word that translates to the above sentiments (see Appendix A). Tourism workers—from airport staff to retail clerks to, assuredly, hotel employees—are told that the Aloha Spirit is Hawai'i's most valuable resource, the magic ingredient that allows Hawai'i to eclipse all other destinations. Being required to say "Aloha!" to every guest is routine. It reminds me of Mr. Roarke instructing his exotic employees, "Smiles, everyone! Smiles!" as the propeller plane approached Fantasy Island. This enforced pleasantry runs the risk of the insincerity that plagues "Have a nice day," which is unfortunate for many reasons, not the least of which is that many kama'āina feel that aloha is a *real* thing, a divine energy that begets a respect for the land and for each other. To residents, aloha is about living in (not spending money in) Hawai'i. But when tourism numbers decline, one of the predominant culprits fingered is a "decline in the Aloha Spirit." In other words, it is the people's fault for not being accommodating enough to outsiders.

Another problem with this official "can't we all get along and drink a Coke" motto is it shuts down the citizens' expression of disharmony. Native Hawaiians—the

people the tourist industry would have you believe are the original and deepest personification of Aloha Spirit—have a lot to be unhappy about, with the loss of their culture, people, and land. But their government tells them that to express their unhappiness would be distinctly un-Hawaiian. How's that for some irony?

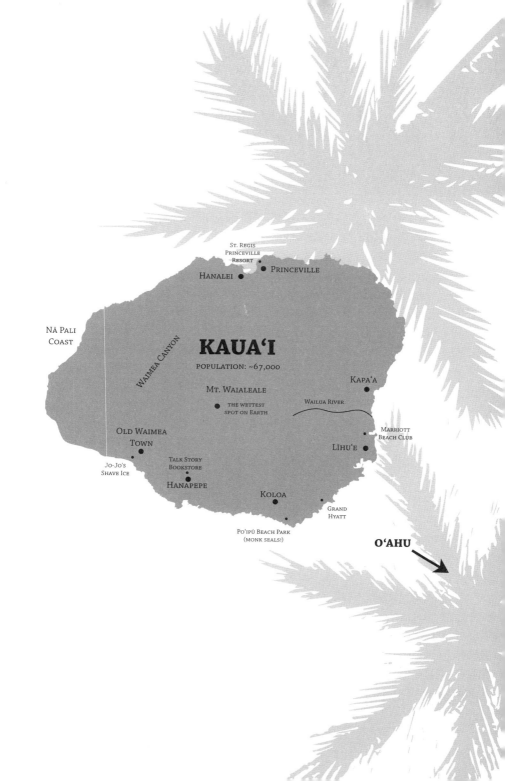

St. Regis
Princeville
Resort

● Princeville

Hanalei ●

Nā Pali
Coast

Waimea Canyon

KAUA'I

POPULATION: ~67,000

Kapa'a

Mt. Waialeale

● THE WETTEST
SPOT ON EARTH

Wailua River

Old Waimea
Town

Marriott
Beach Club

Talk Story
Bookstore

Līhu'e ●

Jo-Jo's
Shave Ice

Hanapepe

Koloa

Grand
Hyatt

Po'ipū Beach Park
(MONK SEALS!)

O'AHU

On the Tail of 'Iniki

O N MY HONEYMOON, I FELL IN LOVE WITH AN ISLAND.
I first set foot on lush Kaua'i in July of 1994. Michael
and I had gotten engaged on October 4th of the previous year, and my mom died exactly three months later on
January 4th. We married at the end of June, with my mom's
face in a frame gracing the altar next to a lit candle that was
supposed to represent her spirit. Michael and I spent most
of our honeymoon on Maui at the familiar InterContinental,
where I eked my way through the six-month anniversary of
my mom's death. We planned to spend the last three days
of our honeymoon on Kaua'i. Only three days, because we'd
never been there and didn't want to be stuck if the Garden
Isle turned out to be too quiet, too boring, too rural for our
twenty-something aesthetic.

Landing at the Lihu'e Airport reminded me of the
Maui airport from my youth: small enough to walk from
one end to the other in less than ten minutes, open-air, and
permeated with the scent of plumeria. The thirty-minute
drive from the airport to the resort town of Po'ipū took
us through Kaua'i's Tree Tunnel, named for the five hundred eucalyptus trees that grow on both sides, arching
up and over into a tangled canopy shading the road. But
the trees were saplings when we came through, allow-
ing the sun to hit and heat the black tar. The trees were

saplings because less than two years earlier on September 11th (what is *with* that date?), Hurricane 'Iniki had raged across Kaua'i, yanking trees and shrubs and ferns and flowers from the earth, stripping away the Garden Island's trademark greenery.

'Iniki began its reign of terror south of Baja on September 6, 1992, as Tropical Depression Eighteen-E. Over the next few days it headed due west, gaining intensity to first become a tropical storm, and then a hurricane. If it had become a tropical storm when it was still in the Eastern Pacific Basin, it might have been branded with a Latin American name, like Aletta or Julio or Tico or Blanca. But because it had crossed into the Central Pacific Basin, the list of names to choose from were Polynesian. This storm was given the name 'Iniki, which is widely reported to mean "piercing wind," but many Hawaiian linguists say it means a "a pinch or sharp bite." Either way, it doesn't sound pleasant.

Not long after gaining its new moniker, 'Iniki spotted Hawai'i. "*Hey, that place looks nice!*" it thought, and made a northwesterly turn towards the islands. 'Iniki's winds whirled faster with a hunger to live up to its name, but its overall movement towards the archipelago slowed. Maybe it needed time to contemplate which island to hit, since each one has something different to offer.

The first and the most southeastern in the chain was the Big Island of Hawai'i. With active volcanoes and beaches and mountains and snow, the Big Island had something for everyone. But if 'Iniki landed there, it might have to contend with the wrath of Pele, the tempestuous goddess of volcanoes. Plus, the island is so damn *big*—perhaps big enough to weaken 'Iniki's power. So it moved on towards crowd-pleasing Maui. The second most-visited and populous island in the state was a tempting spot to make landfall, for sure. As an added bonus, 'Iniki might have been able to take out the three smaller islands off Maui's western shores: Kaho'olawe (just think what a swipe at the US military this could be!), Lāna'i (the Pineapple Isle's resident crop would get whipped into a delicious frenzy), or Molokai (I know, I know—who would want to pillage the Friendly Isle? The thing is, hurricanes are notorious bullies). Maui County would be a hell of a destructive feat. But as a force of nature, 'Iniki possessed eons of wisdom—enough to realize that even though Haleakalā hadn't erupted since the 17th century, it was probably a force you didn't want to fuck with. I mean, its resident demigod, Maui, had lassoed *the frickin' sun*, forcing it to rise in the east. If Maui could control the sun, what wrath might he unleash on a hurricane?

So, the storm moved on. By the morning of September 10th, 'Iniki was only 460 miles south of Honolulu. The island of O'ahu is Hawai'i's third largest in geographic size, but two-thirds of the state's population lives there. Home to the state capitol, Waikīkī Beach, surfing's famed North Shore, and Pearl Harbor, it's also the state's biggest touristic draw. Just think of all the mai tais 'Iniki could whirligig here! The luaus that could be disrupted, the ukuleles splintered, the high-rise hotels brought down, the hundreds of billions of dollars of damage that could be wrought—enough to rival that punk Hurricane

Andrew. But perhaps ʻIniki was irritated by how bad the highway traffic is in Honolulu (the second worst in the entire United States!), or maybe was just turned off by the generic concrete jungle, because it made a sharp turn towards Kauaʻi instead. The Garden Island had a relatively small population—just around 50,000 people on 552 square miles—but it was green and it was quiet and it was old. Mystical. Deciding this was the place, ʻIniki picked up force and became a category 4 hurricane.

A former hairdresser of mine was studying at the University of Hawaiʻi in 1992. She said that when ʻIniki turned away from Honolulu, the students used it as an opportunity to party hard (like they needed an excuse, right?). "Whoo-hoo, we didn't get hit!" they said, and threw hurricane bashes. When they learned of the devastation on Kauaʻi the next day, their hangovers of regret were even greater than from a usual night of partying.

The eastern edge of ʻIniki's eye made landfall during high tide and a full moon, only eight miles from the resort town of Poʻipū. With peak winds reaching 175 miles per hour, ʻIniki ripped up trees and flowers and chickens and electrical poles. Tin roofs flew off buildings and landed on top of cars, crushing them like a meteorological demolition derby. ʻIniki didn't differentiate between multimillion-dollar houses and shacks: it flattened them equally. Even the famed Coco Palms Resort where Elvis had filmed *Blue Hawaii* was destroyed. The eleven-and-a-half-mile-wide eye of ʻIniki spent forty terrifying minutes passing over tiny Kauaʻi, gaining wind strength as it crossed the mountain ridges. ʻIniki left the island at twice the speed it arrived. But the post-vacation malaise hit it fast: by September 13th 'Iniki was no longer a hurricane, and by the September 15th it acquired the sad title of "extra tropical low."

On our honeymoon twenty months later, the Hyatt Regency was the only hotel in Po'ipū to have reopened. The Sheraton wouldn't resume operations until five years after 'Iniki trashed the southwest shore, and two other major hotels were written off entirely. Even though you'd think that would mean the Hyatt could jack up their prices, the opposite was true: in order to encourage tourism, they offered rooms in their fancy resort for well below their normal rate. I think about that sometimes: if it hadn't been for 'Iniki, Michael and I might have stayed somewhere else in Po'ipū, someplace undoubtedly cheaper than the Hyatt, but perhaps someplace less magical, someplace that wouldn't have spoken to my soul so deeply about what it means to recover.

The solid concrete structure of the Hyatt didn't suffer significant storm damage, but 'Iniki's sustained winds of 145 mph and twenty-foot waves had shattered glass, flooded rooms, and ripped the hotel grounds bare. The rest of Po'ipū was still recovering as we drove toward the Hyatt—it was slow, quiet, devoid of crowds—but there were no signs of distress at the resort. Hibiscus and ginger and coconut palms flourished. Black swans glided in placid lagoons. The hotel was shiny, as if it were brand new. Every member of the staff seemed genuinely happy, not just "Aloha!-It's-my-job-to-appear-happy" happy. They had jobs, they had homes, they were alive.

That balmy evening Michael and I sipped overpriced tropical concoctions at the twenty-seven-foot-long koa wood bar while watching a video about the reconstruction of the hotel. The VHS (which the current concierge tells me has since been stolen) compiled home footage of roofs being ripped off houses, boats overturned, helicopters crumpled like discarded soda cans, homes reduced to matchsticks, and tourists huddled in dark hotel basements.

True Hollywood Story side note here: the first *Jurassic Park* movie was filming on Kaua'i when the storm hit. The whole crew—including the stars—huddled in the Lihu'e Westin's basement ballroom along with all the other hotel guests. Crazy camera operators stood near the shore and filmed the twenty-five-foot waves barreling their way until hotel security came along and said, "Yo, get your asses into the shelter."

When the rain and wind ceased and the sun showed its rays, the destruction was clear. Two-thirds of all homes were seriously damaged or destroyed. Roads were impassible, the airport was closed, fishing and tour boats were wrecked. Tourism and all its adjacent industries were destroyed, plunging islanders into massive unemployment. So kama'āina did what humans tend to do in the face of a shared disaster: they all pitched in to help.

Bubba's Burgers hauled their grill to a park, cooked up all the food they had, and gave it away to anyone who needed a meal. GTE Hawaii provided free phone banks, the military provided hot meals, and the county offered free island-wide bus service. Tropical Taco, which had lost its roof, allowed people to sleep in its "taco wagon," a green VW bus. Residents cleared the colossal amount of debris from beaches, and planted new flora. Everyone pitched in to help out everyone else. It was the true nature of Aloha spirit on display: take care of each other, and take care of the land.

Immediately after the storm, the Hyatt offered their entire staff jobs rebuilding the resort. It gave hundreds of people something to do—while getting paid—and helped stave off despair. It was a brilliant move on their part; not only did the Hyatt get their hotel reopened in only six months, waaaaay ahead of all other hotels, they also got to look like good guys while doing it. Super practical and a great PR move, all in one. I can't figure out why the other hotels didn't do the same.

Nearly $2 billion of damage was sustained on Kaua'i. Although President George Bush *Uno* ordered disaster aid much faster than he had for Florida after Hurricane Andrew, he never came to visit the survivors or view the destruction. (Hurricane response is obviously not that family's strong suit.) Four weeks after the storm, 80 percent of Kaua'i still didn't have electricity, and it took ten weeks for power to be restored to the entire island. Residents bathed in waterfalls and streams. One-third of the population was rendered suddenly homeless. Many others lived in badly damaged homes covered by blue tarps. $56 million in agricultural crops were destroyed, and the island lost over $600 million dollars in tourist income the year after the hurricane. Think about how sparsely populated this rural island is and how great the damage was. Think about how much worse the destruction would have been if ʻIniki *had* hit Honolulu instead.

I sat at the koa bar and cried. "Look what happened to this amazing place," I said to Michael. When the video ended, I asked the bartender to replay it from the beginning, and I cried again, and then I returned to my safe hotel room. I was already in love with the island, only twenty-four hours after arriving, equally drawn to its beauty and its ability to survive. Six months after my mom's death, I couldn't foresee the rest of my family's demise. But somehow I knew that I would need Kauaʻi. I would need its wisdom on how to survive.

Da Kine | *Pidgin*

"Pro Tip," offers a travel blog I ran across, "greet people with 'Howzit!' and they'll wonder if you're from the Islands!" Let me disabuse everyone of this notion immediately: a resident mistaking you for kama'aina if you use Pidgin is about as likely as white suburbanites blending seamlessly into the 'hood by hollering "Fo' shizzle my nizzle!"

Hawaiian Pidgin is a creole dialect (*not* slang) that evolved from Filipino, Chinese, Korean, Portuguese, and Hawaiian laborers trying to communicate with each other and the English-speaking plantation owners. It blended words and sounds from all their languages and further developed as the workers' children used it in school. Modern Pidgin ranges from the simple, like ending sentences with "yeah?" (I do this, by the way), to complex dialect that is baffling to the untrained ear: "Ho, get choke mangoes dis yeah, brah!" (I think I heard something about mangoes in there, right?) Like African-American Vernacular English (aka: Ebonics), Pidgin is often characterized as the tongue of the poor and uneducated. As a result, even the most hardcore Pidgin speakers are adept at code-switching, using standard American English in situations where they might be discriminated against for using Hawaiian Creole English.

The irony (there's often irony in colonialism, I'm learning) is that white folks—and especially tourists—think this tongue of the "poor and uneducated" sounds kind of cool, and think that by speaking it, they'll be considered cool. That they'll fit in. When I was a teenager, my local friends used some Pidgin around me, and I picked up a few phrases (stink eye, talk story, chicken skin). It seemed no big deal back then. But in 2012, when it was just me and Michael eating dinner at the Barefoot Bar in Līhuʻe, and the waitress asked me if I was finished with my plate, and I said, "All pau" (all done), she looked at me horribly askance. "Are you *from* here?" she asked.

See, context is everything. When I was sixteen and hanging out with local boys, it was acceptable for me to throw some Pidgin around because I was *with* them. But when it was just me and my haole husband and the clothes and behaviors that identified us as tourists, I'd stepped over a line. It's because Pidgin was and is an essential component of local identity. At its roots, it's a reminder of how so many people came to the Hawaiian melting pot: as indentured servants. And for that waitress it probably meant, "Hey, do you know what it's like to work two jobs to pay rent on a piss-ass house with cockroaches and cane spiders and no air conditioning?"

So, here's the bottom line for us tourists: it's *probably* not an appropriative atrocity to use a *little* Pidgin. But use it with respect, understand where it comes from, and don't be surprised if a local gives you stink eye.

Real Hawaiʻi

THE DRY, DESERTED SOCCER FIELD AT WAIMEA HIGH School wasn't much to look at on Friday afternoon, but it was directly in our view as my husband and I ate shave ice outside JoJo's. And before you get out your red pen: yes, it is "shave" ice, not shaved; there is no "d" missing from the end. The word evolved from Hawaiian Pidgin, and that "no d" thing is a construction seen in many Creole languages. In Belize, for instance, their most common meal is "stew chicken" with beans and rice—not stewed chicken, and not chicken stew. Shave ice is basically a snow cone, but instead of the ice being pulverized, it's shaved off a block by a sharp blade. If done correctly, this apparently gives the ice a sort of fluffy, not crunchy, texture, but most of the shave ice I've sampled (which I assume was done incorrectly) was pretty much still a snow cone with mango and papaya syrup instead of cherry and grape. Michael and I were eating shave ice outside JoJo's on a Friday afternoon, hashing out whether or not we could/would move to Kauaʻi.

Our Pacific Northwest home of Portland is notoriously rainy and gray in the winter, and I am dependably sad. The fluctuating barometric pressure makes my hips and my spine and my jaw hurt. My neural chemistry needs more than the Prozac and high-dosage vitamin D I've been swallowing for years. It needs organic warmth penetrating my arms, my legs, my chest. For my fascia to not be hardened by the cold, but made smooth and pliable and free to move. It aches for my body to be unencumbered by a long-sleeved shirt and a sweater and a heavy jacket and gloves and pants and socks and boots and a hat. I want to be able to leave the house by simply slipping on sandals with my sundress, and then slipping them off again when I return home.

But it's not just the weather that calls me to Kaua'i. Whenever I first spot the island's emerald cliffs through the oval airplane window, breath rises from my core. Air moves up my body, through my chest, to the top of my throat, and then drops over like a waterfall. Tension evaporates from my muscles. It usually takes a day or two on the ground, in the coarse sand and the swirling sea and the plumeria-perfumed air, until I feel like the true version of me. Not the me that isn't pretty enough or thin enough or smart enough or successful enough. Not the me whose whole family died by the time I was forty-four. In Kaua'i, I am the essence of me. This is my Eden.

* * *

Old Waimea Town isn't just the home of JoJo's Shave Ice, but also the landing site for Captain James Cook and his crew, the first white guys to reach the Hawaiian archipelago. This 1778 event is referred to as "First Western Contact" in the Islands, not the "first discovery of Hawai'i," found in history books with a white ethnocentric bias. There are conflicting stories about how the Hawaiians and European sailors interacted, ranging from "the crew was welcomed with generosity and curiosity, the island women giving sex freely" to "the islanders traded sex for iron nails" to "the crew freely took the island women." Overall, though, Cook's first landing in Hawai'i is seen fairly favorably by both sides, and was certainly much sunnier than his final visit to the Islands a year later, when Cook was killed in what is frequently described as a "skirmish" over a small boat. This oft-used word makes it sound as if the incident was a playground name-calling contest that somehow escalated, and not a violent confrontation between a native culture and an interloper.

After First Contact, Waimea Town served as an important shipping and military port and was Kaua'i's commercial and governmental hub for over a century. Nowadays, it's a laid-back town with a population of just over 1,800. A fifty-minute drive from the airport, Waimea has only one plantation-style hotel and one small inn, and is considered about as close to "real Hawai'i" as you can get on Kaua'i.

"Real Hawai'i" is something you hear about a lot: islanders wanting to preserve it, visitors wanting to experience it, but it's hard to say what it *is*, exactly. It's one of those elusive species that's easier to define by what it's not: real Hawai'i is not lū'aus for five hundred tourists with Hawaiian women shaking their grass-covered thangs and men twirling batons of fire. It's not megaresorts with maze-like swimming pools and championship golf courses and boutiques selling $70 flip-flops. It's not Starbucks or Costco or Macy's or a mall. It's not air conditioning. It's not a place where people don't know their neighbors' names, and don't smile or give the shaka to passing cars. It's not rushed, or even on time. And it's certainly not a tour company called "Real Hawaii" that charges $94 per person—$15 extra for a window seat—for a dinner cruise off Waikīkī, where guests are encouraged to join in the Macarena and a conga line. (I'm not at all kidding when I say I cried upon viewing the website for the latter.) Real Hawai'i is not slick or shiny, and it is not trying to be something it's not, because why would you need to be something other than Hawai'i?

Every February Waimea Town hosts a week-long festival that includes a rodeo, a canoe regatta, 'ukulele contests, a triathlon, live storytelling, a softball tournament, food booths, a lei cowboy hat-making competition, and a celebration of King Kaumuali'i, Kaua'i's last king. Michael and I attended it one year and felt like we were crashing someone else's party. No one was rude to us, but no one was friendly, either. There was none of that "Aloha Spirit" the tourist industry likes to bandy about. For that reason, we're always extra aware of our role as outsiders when we're in Waimea. This is their space, not ours.

* * *

Prior to our shave ice pit stop, Michael and I had been in Hanapepe, the next nearest "big" town to Waimea (pop. 2,600). Hanapepe was founded by immigrant entrepreneurs in the late 1800s, when most other island towns were run by the sugar, coffee, and pineapple concerns. Plantation owners paid for passage for laborers from Korea, the Philippines, Japan, China, and Portugal, a practice commonly referred to as "importing"—as if the workers were commodities with no more agency than lumber or rice. The owners segregated them into camps and fields by nationality, hoping the separation would thwart workers from uniting and striking against making $20 per twenty-seven days and living in cockroach-infested barracks.

In the early twentieth century, Japanese and Filipino workers did manage to unite and strike—with a little thanks to Hawai'i's annexation by the US, which, they heard, outlawed slavery and indentured servitude. Hanapepe became the rebels' place of refuge (imagine a Polynesian Mos Eisley, but without the Wookiees. It would be too hot for them there). The ongoing labor conflicts reached their apex with the Hanapepe Massacre of 1924, with sixteen Filipino strikers and four police officers killed. The modern tourist-oriented website for Hanapepe (*Kauai's Biggest Little Town!*) somehow fails to mention this turbulent event.

Today, the main drag of Hanapepe is lined with false-front buildings housing a handful of art galleries, gift shops, restaurants, and snack counters. Every Friday night the Hanapepe Art Walk draws tourists from all over the island, but if you cruise down Hanapepe Road at any other time, you might think you've time-traveled to some ghost town from the Old West. Some food outlets only open for lunch, at least two restaurants only serve dinner on Fridays, and almost all the stores are closed on Sundays. You get the sense that, with the exception of the Friday Night Art walk, this is a locals' town. That if you walked into Unko's Kitchen on Wednesday at noon, it'd be full of construction workers and coffee farmers and delivery truck drivers eating plate lunches of loco moco (that's a hamburger patty and fried egg smothered in gravy, with scoops of white rice and macaroni salad). Few tourists venture into these sorts of local joints, and the ones who do tend to call themselves "adventurous." The less-than-adventurous tourists move on down the road to browse books at Talk Story.

As soon as you walk into Talk Story, one of the owners immediately greets you with, "Welcome to the western-most bookstore in the United States!" The veracity of this salutation largely depends on whether you count the US territory of Guam—which does have a book-store—as part of the United States. Talk Story is one of the last retail businesses as you're heading out of town on Hanapepe Road. The white false front is embellished with red trim and a corrugated tin awning that creates a "hang out and have a lemonade" kind of front porch. Inside, the walls are ketchup red (the high-fructose corn syrup kind, not the all-natural kind) with high-stacked bookshelves in dark brown and light pine. It's pretty much like any other small bookstore in the world that carries new and used books, except for its extensive collection of Hawaiiana: everything from out-of-print textbooks to self-published local poetry to vintage travel brochures and magazines. [Note: I had to hold myself back from dropping nearly one-hundred bucks on the latter, carrying around a stack of plastic-protected leaf-lets and periodicals, only to slowly put them back on the shelves until I ended up with just two: an *Aloha Magazine* from spring 1979, coinciding with my family's first trip to Hawai'i, and a 1982 booklet about volcanoes on the Big Island.]

The owners of Talk Story are a haole couple: Ed, a very quiet guy, and Cynthia, a very talkative woman whose hair routinely changes shades of red and brown. When we first discovered Talk Story they had two store cats, Celeste and Cami (I believe there has since been a "changing of the guards") and, as any bookseller will tell you, the cats are the ones who really run the joint. Celeste wouldn't let anyone pet her white tummy, but she would let Ed stack as many as nine small paperbacks on her rear end when she was lying down.

Over a decade ago, Ed and Cynthia were honey-mooning on Kaua'i and, as their story goes, they never left. All they had with them were two suitcases and $200. They say they never even sent for anything—like their personal belongings, which makes them sound like fugitives from the law. I'd totally believe that they are, except they're pretty public about their story, and it seems like The Man would have caught up with them by now. They supported themselves by buying up tons of used books and other odds and ends around the island, and then reselling them on eBay. About six years into this piecemeal lifestyle, the owner of a building in Hanapepe offered them free rent on a retail space for one month—and one month only. Ed and Cynthia decided to "go for it," and moved their three thou-sand-ish books into the store. When that one month was up, they had enough money to either pay rent for housing, or pay rent on the bookstore.

Ed and Cynthia contemplated what to do while standing on the swinging suspension footbridge that crosses the Hanapepe River. The original rickety bridge was rebuilt after Hurricane ʻIniki ripped it up in 1992, but it still doesn't give the impression of being entirely stable. This feels an apt metaphor for the decision Cynthia and Ed were trying to make: have a place to live, or jump into owning a retail business, a venture that neither of them had any experience with. It's easy from the debt-choked mainland to assume the choice was obvious—go for the roof over your head. But Kauaʻi has a magic all its own, revealed in that crucial moment by a double rainbow arcing over the river. Ed and Cynthia have owned Talk Story ever since.

* * *

My friend Lena and her family were on Kauaʻi in 2015 to scatter her dad's ashes while Michael and I happened to be on island. Her dad had died the previous September of a mantle cell lymphoma that ate away at his body and collapsed his skull. Kauaʻi was his soul-home, too, so Lena and her husband flew from Austin to meet the rest of her family there. One day while we were eating Puka Dogs in Poʻipū, Lena mentioned they'd stopped at Talk Story on their way to Waimea Canyon the day before.

"Did the owner offer you a job?" I asked.

"Running the store for two weeks so they can go to the mainland," Lena said. "How did you know that?"

The previous year Cynthia had offered Michael a job running a second, yet-to-be-opened Talk Story location in Līhu'e. She proposed this job about five minutes after meeting us, knowing little more than Michael was a bookseller in Portland. She reinforced a few times that she was *serious* in her offer.

"I have a good feeling about you," she said. "Sometimes you just know about people, and I just know about you."

Cynthia was a quirky fairy godmother granting my most fevered wish. How many times had we wistfully said, "If only there was a bookstore we could run on Kaua'i?" Just think how perfect our lives could be in this gentle land that always relaxed our bodies and fulfilled our souls. Sunshine nearly year-round, none of the SAD and requisite high-dosage vitamin D supplementation of the Pacific Northwest. No aching joints when the cold winds blew and the barometric pressure rose, making us feel twenty-five years older than we were. That's what Kaua'i promised: a youthful ease I'd lost along with the deaths of my mom, my dad, and my brother.

"We've thought about moving here," I told Cynthia while Michael browsed the stacks. This should have been my first clue that I was more invested in her offer than he was. "But it would be hard to leave our friends." I knew I didn't function well without real-life connections, and the loneliness might cause a darkness even the sunshine couldn't erase.

"They'll come visit you all the time!" she said. "We see our friends and family now more than we did when we lived on the mainland."

"Maybe," I said. "But it's so expensive to live here."

"Where did you hear that?" Cynthia asked.

"Pretty much everywhere," I said, confused by her question. It seemed akin to someone asking where you'd heard that the world was round. "Housing costs are so high."

The ocean-view condo we were renting for $232 a night was on the market for $800,000 and had an additional home owner's association fee of $1,170 *a month*. The HOA fee alone was more than the monthly mortgage for our house in Portland. Our 1,200-square-foot tract house wasn't fancy by any stretch of the imagination, and *maybe* could fetch $240,000 because of its desirable location near a cute neighborhood and in a good school district. That would hardly buy you a shack in ritzy Poʻipū. In the more "affordable" Līhuʻe—where the new bookstore would be—a place similar to our home would start at around $485,000.

"You don't spend as much time inside here, so you need less," Cynthia said. "Everyone lives outdoors."

I knew I was coming off as a Negative Nelly, but there were well-researched reasons we'd not previously cut the cord to the mainland. "But food is so expensive."

"That's just a myth," she said.

"Well…" My speech was getting slower, "I've been to the grocery store." I'd seen that a quart of milk at Kōloa Big Save costs the same as a *gallon* at Safeway on the mainland. Not that Michael and I drink milk —we're both slightly lactose intolerant. But as a weird artifact from post-WWII consumer days, the price of milk is a signifier of a location's cost of living. And Hawaiʻi's cost of goods and services is 120 percent higher than the national average, the most expensive in the country.

This may seem obvious, but most food and household goods used in Hawai'i need to be shipped halfway across the Pacific Ocean. And thanks to the Jones/Merchant Marine Act of 1920 (there's always some arcane law from the 1920s, isn't there?), these products sometimes need to be shipped a full ocean and a *half* just to get to Hawai'i. That's because the Jones Act dictates that all ships carrying goods between American ports must be built in the United States, be 75 percent owned by a US company, fly a US flag, and use a US crew. What this means practically is that if a Chinese-owned ship travels from Taiwan to Los Angeles (carrying TVs, apple juice, t-shirts, soy sauce, etc.), it can't unload goods in Honolulu along the way. It has to unload in LA, then have those same goods reloaded onto a US ship bound for Honolulu. And here's the super expensive kicker: Hawai'i exports less than half of what it imports, so there's no way to recoup the money for the return trip. Well, except for charging super-high shipping rates.

Hawai'i also has no natural coal or oil reserves, so electricity and gas is all shipped in. This makes electricity in Hawai'i the most expensive in the nation, costing 33.2 cents per kilowatt hour (the second-most expensive is New York State, at an average of 18.1 cents). Gasoline is $0.50 to $1.00 per gallon more than on the mainland. If the idea that it's expensive to live in Hawai'i is a "myth," then it had yet to be dispelled by any data approximating "facts."

"You just grow your own food!" Cynthia-the-Optimist said.

Never mind that I'm the sort of hypocritical carnivore who would languish in bed for a week with the existential flu if I was required to chop off a chicken's head or put a bullet between a cow's eyes. And let's pretend that I don't hate gardening and suck at it. What about the items we can't grow in our own backyard? Like corn flakes. Dark chocolate Linder Balls. Shredded Parmesan cheese. Tortilla chips, mustard, maple syrup, vanilla-flavored almond milk for Michael's coffee, and those all-natural sausages he likes for breakfast? Those are just food items, and don't even start to account for the cost of light bulbs, toilet paper, laundry detergent, shampoo, and toothpaste. Et cetera. That's the reality of real Hawai'i, too: $5 cornflakes, $10 light bulbs, and $15 Tide. It's why so many residents work two or three jobs to afford rent and feed their family—never mind the dream of owning a home.

But we told Cynthia we'd think about it—I don't know if Ed had any idea she'd made this offer to us—and left her with our contact information. "You can e-mail us through our webpage," she said.

* * *

We drove westward to JoJo's, where we sat outside enjoying our cold, fruity delights. A few other tourists in shorts and sandals and T-shirts sat nearby. I felt special compared to them, chosen, because we might actually live there. We might become a part of real Hawai'i.

"We could do it for just one year," I said to Michael. "Just to get the bookstore started."

The elements that usually send mainlanders fleeing back—the cost of living and island fever—would be temporary.

"What about the cats?" Michael asked. Hawai'i recognizes the fragility of their isolated ecosystem, and bringing in a new disease—especially rabies—could be disastrous. All pets, even our cats who never go outside, have to stay in quarantine for 120 days when first arriving in the state.

"They have a new program that's only five days if you meet certain criteria," I said. "Quick release," they call it, as if they were fish being caught for sheer enjoyment.

The new five-day rule involves a complicated timetable for when your pet gets multiple rabies shots in relation to each other and when they arrive on the island (two vaccinations administered more than 30 days apart, with the last one not less than 90 days before arriving on island; a blood sample tested at the Kansas State University not more than 36 months and not less than 120 days before arriving—wait, what?). We'd need a spreadsheet and some sort of computer software to determine the perfect timing.

That's when Michael told me that this whole thing—the idea of moving to Kaua'i—was stressing him out. Thinking about it exhilarated me! The change, the excitement, the finally being able to say: *I did it. I lived in Hawai'i.* To be more than a derided tourist. To be legitimate. To be real. But Michael didn't see that. He saw how our world had been rocked by nothing but change—seriously terrible, unwelcome change—for the past several years, as we'd navigated the illnesses and deaths of my dad and brother and the legal morass that ensued. But above and beyond the cost and the cats and the change, Michael had one very fine reason to not take the job, even for—especially for—one year: it would be a *drag*.

Starting a new retail business requires long hours, inventory, bookkeeping, sales, marketing, the holiday rush, the barren months of no holidays, the desperate attempts to avoid red ink, the forever-smile when a potential customer wanders into the store. It's a constant web of worry and work. "That's the worst part of running a business," Michael said. "And we'd have to live in Līhu'e or Kapa'a, which we *hate*, and why would we want to come to Hawai'i to just be stressed out?"

It might even ruin Kaua'i for us. The island where we escaped to heal from the wounds in our hearts and heads might transform from our savior to our oppressor.

By the time we got back to the condo, my stomach was cramping from the realities of the high-fructose corn syrup and yellow dyes #5 and #6 in my mango shave ice. I sat in the living room, looking out on the ocean, listening to the waves, surfing on my laptop. Earlier in the day I'd posted on Facebook: *Holy shit-balls. A local bookstore owner just offered Michael a job running her new store in Lihue.* A few hours later, I had fifty comments saying things like, "Do it!" and "Heaven!" and "What are you waiting for?"— all understandable reactions when you don't have to consider the logistics and consequences of a move to the most expensive and isolated state in the country.

I was sad that night, and not just because of my shave ice stomachache. We were tourists, and that's all we'd ever be. The word felt so derogatory, as if the island was just some one-night stand that we used up and threw away after it fulfilled a transient desire. As if all we cared about was the shiny façade, and not the more complicated reality. Even the Hawai'i Tourism Authority avoids the word tourist, choosing "visitors" instead. It's friendly, and it implies a bilateral agreement between the people of Hawai'i and those only coming for a short stay. Visitors are welcomed—perhaps even invited—and will mind their manners like any proper guest does. This is the message the Hawai'i Tourism Authority telegraphs with an almost Big Brother-like fervor.

When we returned to Portland, I emailed Cynthia and Ed and told them how much we liked meeting them and the cats. I reminded them who we are—the bookseller from Portland and his author wife—but didn't mention the job offer. I was curious to see if Cynthia would bring it up. I didn't hear back from them. The next time we went in the store, ten months later, neither of them talked to us at all, not even to welcome us to the westernmost bookstore in the United States. I wondered if the knowledge that we wouldn't actually move there, that we were poseurs, acted as an invisibility cloak that erased us from their view.

After the realization that we would never be kama'āina, I started calling myself a "frequent visitor." I hoped the modifier would give me some legitimacy so others would know my relationship with Hawai'i was not just a fling, but a deep, abiding love. But no matter how frequently I visit this place, these islands, the depth of this love can never be the same as someone who has lived on the 'āina, who has paid the price for paradise and nonetheless decided to stay.

Da Kine | 'Ukulele

A 'UKULELE'S SPRIGHTLY STRUMMING IS THE EMBLEM-atic sound of the Islands. Hula is the dance, pineapple the fruit, and surfing the sport that paints Hawaiian life—lilting, fun, sweet, and slightly exotic. Ironically, the 'ukulele isn't actually Hawaiian—in the sense that it didn't *originate from* Hawai'i. The diminutive four-stringer made its way to Hawai'i via Portugal. The Portuguese made their way to Hawai'i when a blight on the 1877 citrus crop triggered massive unemployment, causing men to emigrate for work. It's hard for me, a modern middle-class American, to comprehend traveling eight thousand miles to one of the most isolated archipelagos in the world for a crap-ass paying job, but travel they did: from 1878 to 1912, twenty-five thousand Portuguese—mainly from Madeira and the Azores—came to Hawai'i as contract laborers. They brought their families and their food and their cavaquinhos, the 'ukulele prototype.

Folks of Portuguese ancestry now comprise 4.3 percent of Hawai'i's population, but their cultural influence is disproportionately greater. Portuguese sausage, malasadas (yummy doughnuts!), and the 'ukulele are intrinsic to Hawai'i. While commercialism (and vaudeville) belittled the 'ukulele in the mid-twentieth century, cultural practitioners like the great musician Israel Kamakawiwo'ole (affectionately called Bruddah Iz) restored its dignity and artistry in the 1990s. Iz, himself, is a symbol of real

Hawai'i, Native Hawai'i, unspoiled Hawai'i. That he is forever linked with an instrument not endemic to Hawai'i isn't so much irony, but evidence that modern Hawai'i is defined by its multitudes.

HILTON WAIKOLOA
VILLAGE

MAUNA KEA
(SNOW!)

HILO

ISLAND OF HAWAI'I
(THE BIG ISLAND)

KAILUA-KONA

THE EASTERN RIFT ZONE

SITE OF CAPTAIN
COOK'S DEMISE

VOLCANOES
NATIONAL PARK

VOLCANO VILLAGE/
KILAUEA LODGE
VOLCANO HOUSE HOTEL

VISITOR OVERLOOK

HALEMA'UMA'U CRATER

Volcanoes, Palm Trees, and Privilege: The Self-Contained Paradise of the Hawaiian Resort

To those who have seen Hawaiʻi, I can promise many special new delights on a return visit.
—JAMES MICHENER, FROM A MAGAZINE AD
FOR UNITED AIRLINES, 1980

My family's first trip to Hawaiʻi wasn't exactly enchanting (let us recall the flat tire, the diarrhea, and the United Airlines strike), yet my dad somehow believed James Michener's promise that a return visit would bring us new delights. In 1981, my dad, brother and I returned (via coach class) to Maui, now one less, as my parents had divorced soon after our first failed trip. A friend of my dad's offered us his condo in Kīhei at the Haleakala Shores complex on southwest Maui. My dad accepted the offer, sight unseen.

The Kīhei condo turned out to be small and hot and dark and draped in brown and avocado green. I slept on

a pullout couch in the living room. There was no air conditioning, so we left the windows open at night. Spiders
and flying creatures invaded. Dead leaves floated in the
small, shady pool. Looking into our near future, I wondered who was going to grocery shop and cook and clean.
My dad paid other people to do it back home. I lived with
my mom in a more modest reality that included cooking
for ourselves and the full range of domestic chores, but I
certainly wasn't going to do them *for* my dad and brother
on vacation.

On our first day in the small, dark condo, my dad let
Steve, who wasn't even sixteen, borrow the car. He drove
us two and a half miles south to the InterContinental
Hotel in Wailea, an oceanfront resort with manicured
lawns and winding sidewalks and three swimming pools,
none of which were garnished with dead leaves. The
InterContinental opened in 1976 as Wailea's first hotel,
so it was still pretty shiny when Steve and I first wandered its grounds. Guests played Frisbee and volleyball,
and enjoyed sandwiches and frothy drinks ferried to them
by sun-kissed waitresses in floral skirts.

"We have to convince Dad to move us here," Steve said.
"We can't stay in that condo."

Spending our vacation at Haleakala Shores wasn't like
going to my dad's weekend condo in Colorado Springs,
which was also small and horribly decorated. We'd sometimes invite a bunch of friends, and my dad might bring
a girlfriend along (because wow, it's every woman's dream
to spend a romantic weekend in Colorado Springs with
a gaggle of teenagers!). We'd order pepperoni pizza from

the joint next door, and it was no big deal if one of us had to sleep on the couch or even the floor. That was just a *weekend*, an extended slumber party—not a vacation. Colorado Springs made no promises of paradise, after all. But TV and movies and glossy magazine ads had long ago sold us on the promise that a Hawaiian vacation was supposed to be Elysium on Earth, that there would be no dead leaves or invading insects or avocado green.

I couldn't imagine how we'd convince our dad to spend money on the InterContinental. Surely it was expensive, and definitely more expensive than our borrowed Kīhei condo. Our dad had *some* money, but did he have that much? If he did have that much, why would he have agreed to the bargain-rate condo in the first place? Maybe he didn't want to insult his friend by turning down the generous offer. Maybe a piece of my dad was still the poor boy from southern Colorado who knew that any condo in Maui for a week was a treasure—a lesson his kids weren't so clear on.

"Let me handle it," Steve said. "I can convince him."

When we returned to Haleakala Shores, Steve told Dad that we'd driven to the InterContinental and walked around. "Everyone was laughing and having fun," Steve said. "We were watching some kids our age playing volleyball and they asked us to join. We told them we weren't staying at the hotel, and they said it would be against the rules to play so we just had to stand there and watch." He managed to even *whine* a little when he said it.

All it took was that one lie: Steve playing on my dad's guilt that his children's desires weren't being met, the opposite of his poor, violent, loss-filled childhood. We moved to the InterContinental later that day, Steve and my dad in one room and me adjoining (rooms 6410 and 6412). We returned two or three times a year for the next few years, to those same rooms, as my dad built a housing subdivision in Kīhei. That's how the Hawaiian resort became the setting, scene, plot, and character for my coming of age.

Society's Winter Paradise
Sophisticates enticed by the bizarre...have learned that Hawaii is just a few days away.
—Hawaii Tourist Bureau newspaper ad, 1929

The Hawaiian resort hotel is so engrained in my experience that I practically assume they were all spewed from ancient volcanoes, molten amorphisms hardened and shaped by eons of water and by wind. But, of course, Hawaiian resorts had to be conceptualized. They had to be constructed. Over the last hundred years they have evolved, growing and receding and then returning with new shapes and forms. In 2017, they have almost stopped being built—which is not to say they are in danger of going extinct; on the contrary, they continue to thrive and mostly likely always will, because the Hawaiian resort is the emblem, the epitome, of paradise.

In 2015, 8.6 million people visited Hawai'i, showering the state with $15.2 billion. About 54 percent of these visitors stayed exclusively in hotels. That may not sound like an impressive majority until you consider that it's nearly *four times* more people than those who stay in condos, the next most-booked lodging choice. Not surprisingly, 72 percent of people who stay in hotels are on vacation.

In case you're wondering why and how these statistics are remotely interesting, consider this: staying in a hotel is much more expensive than staying in a condo. Condos, generally, cost less per night—especially on a per-bed basis. A garden view thousand-square-foot two-bedroom (one king and two twins) condo in Wailea Grand Champions Resort—that has two pools and a hot tub— costs $200 a night during shoulder season. At the Wailea Marriott one mile away, the cheapest room—a garden view with two queen beds, measuring a cozy 437 square feet—costs $519, including the daily resort and parking fees. Meals also cost significantly less in a condo than a hotel (I refer you to the Marriott's $18 pancakes—no sausage or bacon—and $17 hot dogs, before tax and tip).

So, visitors, especially families, choose to stay in hotels for reasons that appear to have little to do with budget or spaciousness. They are looking for an entire experience, one that is lushly landscaped and bug free, with elaborate swimming pool playgrounds consuming half a million gallons of water, with Zen-like spas selling coconut-and mango-scented shampoo and lotions, and one that includes someone else assuming the burden of cooking, cleaning, carrying anything that might be deemed cumbersome, bringing fresh towels upon command, and how about those employees who walk around the pool handing out sun-screen and frozen pineapple chunks and cool washcloths in case that tropical sun gets to be too much?

Those 54 percent of visitors staying exclusively in hotels suggest that the luxurious escape from the drudgery of everyday life is as much a part of the Hawaiian tourist product as the ocean and palm trees and warm breezes and dazzling sunsets. But how—when and where—did that expectation begin?

In the early nineteenth century, Island lodgings were mostly taverns for whaling crews, providing bars, billiards, and beds. It was pretty rough stuff for the genteel visitors arriving in increasing numbers from San Francisco and Great Britain by mid-century—some adventurers, some artists, some invalids seeking the sun and saltwater cure—so enterprising haoles converted their homes into inns. These large colonial-style houses boasted a parlor and dining room on the ground floor, bedrooms and wash-rooms on the second. Open-air lānais were usually part of the package, although in this architectural style it's impossible to not think the word "veranda."

I haven't found any mention of Native Hawaiians providing lodging for visitors at this time to capitalize on the outside interest in their homeland. Their houses, for the most part, were pretty simple by Western stan-dards, hand-constructed of wood and grass with modest furnishings. Possibly these digs weren't up to snuff for the haole visitors. But I suspect there's something else at play: the idea that Hawaiians were not as *civilized* as haoles. Although early nineteenth-century missionaries had successfully "tamed the savages," Hawaiians were still regarded as distinctly *other*. The missionaries assumed the natives would descend back into their heathen ways if they didn't endeavor to uphold their purity every day. The very nature of having been taught to read and write and wear clothes and worship God (of the uppercase) by haoles created a paternalistic relationship. This would always place them below white folks on the colonial social stratum, and I'm guessing that staying in the homes of people considered beneath you was just not done.

By the mid-1800s, more wealthy white people were showing up in Honolulu than there were acceptable accommodations to be had. I find it mind-boggling that folks got on a steamship and spent one to two weeks crossing the ocean without knowing where they'd sleep when they arrived. Before I make reservations—reservations!—I spend a psychotic amount of time reading TripAdvisor reviews and combing through pictures on hotel and VRBO websites and virtually walking the neighborhood via Google Street View. Clearly, the internet has made us less adventurous, less brave, less willing to throw ourselves unto the breach.

In 1869, Prince Alfred (aka: the Duke of Edinburgh) was amid a five-year cruise around the world—and a year outside an assassination attempt in Australia (!)—when he stopped in Honolulu. The prevailing legend holds that couldn't find lodging aside from a shabby room above a disreputable saloon, and King Kamehameha V was so embarrassed that he demanded a hotel be built to befit visiting dignitaries. This story seems a little far-fetched, seeing how Honolulu was home to the royal 'Iolani Palace, which probably could dust off an extra bedroom for the son of Queen Victoria. It's not as if Prince Alfred arrived undetected on a raft in the middle of the night. Certainly, someone must have noticed a frigate of the British Royal Navy in the harbor. And, if not, when he came ashore, couldn't he just identify himself and ask to be taken to the Palace? Or, upon learning of his presence, wouldn't rich haoles be falling all over themselves to host him in their homes? I'm pretty sure that's actually what happened. In the verbosely titled *The Cruise of His Royal Highness the Duke of Edinburgh, K.G., Round the World in H.M.S. "Galatea," Catalogue of Water-Colour Sketches and Drawings of the Cruise*, is a description of a sketch (although not the sketch itself) by N. Chevalier identified as a "view from the verandah of the residence prepared for, and occupied by, the Duke of Edinburgh, while staying at Honolulu; the 30th of July 1869."

Whatever the inciting incident, the Hawaiian government opened the Hawaiian Hotel in 1871. It boasted forty-two bedrooms with luxurious furniture, linens, and mattresses. The grounds were landscaped with grass, palm trees, passionflower, and other local flora. While that might seem sort of obvious—since the hotel was in Hawai'i and all—the salient point is that the grounds were *landscaped*. Trees and flowers and shrubs and grass were planted where they had not previously existed, and needed to be fertilized and watered and otherwise maintained. This deliberate—and resource-intensive—horticulture would eventually become a feature of all Hawaiian resorts.

The original budget for the hotel was $46,000, but it ended up costing $120,000. I'd love to translate how much that is in today's money, but my most-reliable online inflation calculator doesn't go back that far. Let's just assume it was a *lot*, especially since a small kingdom was footing the bill. King Kamehameha V died the year after the Hawaiian Hotel opened, and his advisers who okayed the building cost—Charles Coffin Harris and John Mott-Smith (a *dentist*)—not so coincidentally lost their jobs.

Even though the hotel was financed by Hawai'i, its management was not Hawaiian. It was leased to and run by a Swede named Allen Herbert. I don't know if this is because the King was aware of the "otherness" of his own people, and assumed/knew travelers would be disinclined to stay in a hotel managed by Hawaiians. Or perhaps he figured that because capitalism was not an innate aspect of Hawaiian society, his own people wouldn't know how to run a business. Or maybe he and his royal predecessors had depended upon haoles for so long that it didn't occur to him to do business any other way. (King Kamehameha I, for instance, employed two haole war advisors who supplied him with the cannon that insured his military victory over all the islands.) Regardless of the original reason for not including Hawaiians in the management of the Hawaiian Hotel, I wonder if the trajectory of the people and their land would have been different if they'd been invited to participate? Maybe not. Most likely, foreigners would still enforce their economic desires on the Islands. Still, it's always nice to be asked.

The rate to stay at The Hawaiian Hotel was $3 per day, or $15 per week, and I get the impression that was not considered cheap back then. But intrepid world traveler Isabella Bird wrote, "…such a kindly, open-handed system prevails that I am not conscious that I am paying anything!… Hospitality seems to take possession of and appropriate one as soon as one enters its never-closed door, which is on the lower verandah. [See? Another veranda!] Everywhere, only pleasant objects meet the eye." The service was so seamless, she wrote, her constitution so replenished, that she could let any and every worry just fade away. And that sounds a lot like the first Hawaiian resort.

Think of Swimming off Waikiki in the moonlight…think of strangely delicious new foods to eat, new sights to see, new sports to enjoy!
—AD FOR MATSON LINE CRUISE SHIP IN THE MALOLO, C.1938

Modern Waikīkī holds the dubious honor of being iconic of Hawai'i, its name and beaches the state's most recognized touristic locale, and yet weirdly unlocatable by many mainland Americans. Lots of folks I've talked to who have never been to Hawai'i think Waikīkī (and Honolulu, the state capitol it's a neighborhood of) are on the island of Maui—not southeastern O'ahu. It kind of makes sense, since the island you hear most about is Maui, and the city you hear most about is Honolulu. They must be in the same place, right? For the longest time, Honolulu and its famous Waikīkī Beach were destinations unto themselves, and there seemed no reason to mention, apparently, that they're on Oʻahu. (As for Pearl Harbor, even I often forget where, exactly, it is in relation to Honolulu and Waikīkī— which is, to the left.)

Like many island locales, Waikīkī was once a chill settlement occupied by fishponds and taro patches and the people who tended to them. That took a bloody turn when Kamehameha stormed its shores in 1795 and massacred hundreds of soldiers during his quest to unite all the islands under his rule. By the mid-1800s, Waikīkī had become a vacation playground for Hawaiian royalty where, according to waikiki.com (*Welcome to Paradise!*), they enjoyed "moonlight horseback rides, thrilling canoe races, and carefree romps in the ocean."

As a once-history major and a fan of semantics, I get tangled in that language. What was unique about these moonlight horseback rides—how were they specific to Waikīkī and its aura? What was particularly thrilling about these canoe races, compared to canoe races at other beaches among commoners? And what, exactly, does "carefree romps in the ocean" mean? Maybe I'm being prurient, but it's hard to escape the sexual connotations of the word romp. The activities and the way they're described conjure an exotic, untamed otherness, one that entices modern travelers to escape the restrained banality of their plebeian lives. This description appears on a modern travel website—not a historical or academic one—meaning its purpose is to encourage tourism. It promises the reader: "You can be like royalty and have a thrilling, carefree time on Waikīkī, that may include random romps." It's not a stretch to imagine their unofficial slogan: "What happens in Waikīkī stays in Waikīkī."

These days, eighty hotels populate the less than one square mile of Waikīkī. Some of them scrape the sky, most of them house pools and restaurants and bars; some also boast nightclubs and spas and entire shopping malls. If you take away the beach and add casinos, you pretty much have Las Vegas. And like Las Vegas, I used to think everyone should visit Waikīkī at least once—it's that iconic a piece of popular culture. It's the stomping grounds of Elvis and Gidget and Sinatra, Steve McGarrett, Thomas Magnum and the *Brady Bunch*. People who can't tell you the names of any of the Hawaiian Islands, including Oʻahu, can probably identify a picture of Waikīkī. For better or worse, Hawaiʻi and Waikīkī are interchangeable in the American mind.

Since my husband had never visited the emblematic locale, we took a one-night side trip there on the way back from Kauaʻi in 2000. We didn't stay at the esteemed Royal Hawaiian Hotel, since it's old and we're modernists, and because the cost was above our pay grade. The hotel was built specifically for rich people, after all. After Hawaiʻi was annexed as a US territory in 1898, travelers were extra reassured that it was a safe and civilized locale, and rich tourists set across the Pacific in droves. When Matson luxury steamships pulled into Honolulu harbor, passengers threw coins overboard and watched local boys dive into the water to retrieve them. It wasn't just charity—as if that wouldn't be condescending enough—but entertainment to the arriving mainlanders. Look at those brown boys dive for the pennies and nickels we throw to them. Isn't that something?

Hoteliers caught on that pleasure travelers wanted to stay at the beach, so they drained the swamp (I'm being literal here: Waikīkī was actually a marsh) and built the Moana Hotel in 1901 and then the Royal Hawaiian in 1927. The Pepto-pink Royal Hawaiian boasted four hundred rooms, doubling the total number of guest rooms available in Waikīkī. To give you some perspective on how quaint that is, there are currently *thirty thousand* rooms in Waikīkī. In addition to each room at the Royal Hawaiian having its own bathroom—that was a really big deal back then—individual lānais opened either to the lushly landscaped gardens or a view of the Pacific. Visitors included the rich (Rockefellers, Fords, and Roosevelts) and the famous (Chaplin, Temple, Pickford, and Fairbanks). The lobby boys were dressed in Cathayan costumes, because…I guess it made rich folks feel particularly doted upon if they pretended their servants were Chinese?

Prior to WWII, Pan Am was the only airline flying from the US to Hawai'i, on—I shit you not—flying boats. The clippers were more airplane than boat, in that they flew for nineteen hours of the trip between San Francisco and Honolulu, and used their boat-like capacity for takeoff and landing in water. The body of Boeing's 314 Clipper was nearly as wide as today's 747, but only carried twenty-five passengers. My usually super-smart husband had a hard time understanding how a plane could be *that* big and hold so *few* passengers and fly for *nineteen* hours without a fuel stop ("I'm guessing it had to be that big to hold all the extra fuel," I suggested). There was no such thing as coach or economy fare on the Clipper—it was first class all the way, baby! And not first class like first class is now (Gee, a meal and a blanket? Thanks a bunch), but first class like on the *Titanic*: a dining room with real silver and china, a VIP captain's table, sleeping berths, and a bridal suite. A *one-way* ticket from San Francisco to Honolulu cost $248, the equivalent of $4,000 now. It's not like the masses could afford such a journey, and the Moana and the Royal were sufficient to house the rarified travelers.

Then the Royal Hawaiian took a weird turn during WWII—not that I can judge what a *non*-weird turn looks like after your town is blitzed by a foreign enemy. The hotel became R&R quarters for military men on leave. Not just high-ranking officers, but all grades, and those guys *trashed* the Pink Palace. They carved their initials into the hand-crafted koa woodwork, put out their cigarettes on the lush upholstery, and I can only imagine what they did to the oriental rugs. After the war, the Royal required a $2 million sprucing to get it back up to snuff.

After WWII, United and Northwest Airlines gained permission to fly to Hawai'i, and actual landplanes started making the route. Planes got bigger, the Honolulu Airport runways got longer, flights from the US got faster, and it was all cheaper. More visitors = more need for hotels = more entrepreneurs seeing a way to make money. Hotels shot up everywhere in Waikīkī, with no vision or plan beyond the draining of the swamp. It wasn't until 1976 that a master plan was introduced to help tame development and establish a "Hawaiian sense of place." I hate to break it to them, but that horse was so far out of the fucking barn by that time that it was on its way to Tahiti.

For Michael's first visit to Waikīkī, we stayed at the Hilton Hawaiian Village and, let me say, it wouldn't be too far off to replace the word "Village" with "Metropolis." The Hilton is staged on twenty-two acres, which sounds spacious until you consider the complex consists of *seven* towers (two are timeshare condos), the highest of which is forty stories tall. There are six pools, three spas, ninety shops, and twenty restaurants (although the hotel's official tally of on-site restaurants includes an Orange Julius, two Starbucks, and a Round Table Pizza, which sorta feels like cheating). The hotel routinely serves 6,000 guests a day, requiring a staff of 1,700. That twenty-two acres gets pretty claustrophobic pretty fast.

Anytime Michael and I dared to navigate the lobby, there were a variety of Polynesian sideshows swirling around us. I could swear there was a man riding a unicycle while swallowing a flaming sword and twirling a cat on top of a spinning plate, but this is probably more of a metaphor for how the whole atmosphere felt. A couple of times we couldn't even find the right elevator bank for our tower. ("Wait, does this take us to the Aliʻi Tower or the Rainbow Tower? Oh my god, how did we end up all the way over at the Diamond Head Tower?") This was our experience of spending only *one night* at the hotel.

Michael and I snapped pictures of each other on the lānai, with the iconic white sand beach extending below us and Diamond Head crater glittering in the distance. By pop culture standards, we'd experienced "the most Hawaiian" thing about Hawai'i. But the whole environment was such a whir that I can't remember stopping to talk with one local, to look them in their eyes, to admire the Hawaiian art and artifacts staged throughout the grounds, to read and learn from the interpretive plaques, to have any experience that wasn't constructed for the sole purpose of generating revenue by fulfilling tourists' (highly subjective) expectation of paradise. But the portraits of us backed by Diamond Head were proof that I'd done it: I'd forced my husband to go to Waikīkī Beach, because "everyone has to go there once." It took me years to live that down.

So close...so easy to reach...so moderate in cost to sail or fly into the sunshine and enticement of Hawaii
—Hawai'i Visitors Bureau Ad, circa 1955

In the 1950s a man named George Sumner did what no one had ever done in Hawai'i: planned an entire resort community. Sumner was president of Amfac, whose subsidiary, Pioneer Mill, owned four hundred acres of shrubland and cane fields on northwest Maui. The land also happened to be fronted by two-and-a-half-mile-long Ka'anapali Beach, which was, as it turned out, too delicious to leave undeveloped. Sumner looked to Waikīkī not so much for the inspiration in planning the Ka'anapali

Resort, but more as a cautionary tale. He envisioned Ka'anapali as less dense, more luxurious, and completely self-contained. His concept was a tropical paradise (there's that word again!) that tourists wouldn't need or want to leave. He, and whoever he leased land to, would be in command of shaping a visitor's entire experience, image, and understanding of Hawai'i, setting precedent for all Island resorts for the next fifty years.

There was just one teeny tiny problem with Sumner's plan: a highway ran right through what should've/could've been prime hotel property along the beach. The coastal highway had recently been extended through Ka'anapali to the tune of $120,000 ($1,064,792.65 in today's economy). Sumner's master resort plan was so enticing that the Maui Board of Supervisors agreed to move the highway further inland at a cost of *$1 million* mid-century dollars. This sounds like the most absurd gambling venture ever, with such long-shot odds that only someone very desperate, or very rich, could afford to make the bet. It's not clear that Maui was desperate, exactly, but its leaders were well aware that they were missing out on tourist dollars. At the time, the island was a one-day side trip, maybe an overnighter, for most visitors to Hawai'i. Hotels were few and far between and either catered to the very wealthy or the practically indigent. But in the 1950s, America birthed this thing called "the middle class," and Maui had yet to reach into its pockets.

While Ka'anapali was being built, a makeshift airstrip emerged in the midst of a cane field. My friend Edie's husband operated Pacific Flight Service, an interisland commuter, and routinely flew over the muckety-mucks involved in the development and planning of the resort. One frequent passenger he struck up a friendship with was Robert Trent Jones, Sr., the esteemed golf course designer. Every morning for nine months, Edie was flown from Oʻahu to Kaʻanapali, where she worked in her husband's office all day ("We didn't have phone lines, so I'd communicate with the Oʻahu office by teletype," she said, prompting Michael to rush to Google for an image of a teletype machine), then be flown back in the evening. The airstrip was so narrow that the airplane's wings brushed stalks of sugar cane during takeoff and landing. Weirdly, there's no record of Pacific Flight Service on the internet or in books. Only on a TripAdvisor forum did I find this message from someone named Gail S:

> *In 1965 I worked for Pacific Flight Service, an inter island charter service. They had regular flights to Kaanapali and as an employee (parts department), I took advantage of a free flight with my girlfriend. It was a scary landing on that field, seems like it was cut in the middle of a plantation. It was a short hot walk to the hotel and the beach.*

The hotel she refers to is the Sheraton, which (finally) opened in 1963. It boasted 212 rooms on fifteen acres atop a lava cliff. The *Chicago-Sun Times* referred to it as an "upside-down hotel" because you entered the lobby from the top of the cliff alongside the road, and then took an elevator down to the rooms, the pool, and the ocean. Kauaʻi's St. Regis Princeville Resort is constructed the same way, and I find it disorienting and slightly annoying for no particular reason, other than it goes against my psychology of what a hotel *is*. The Sheraton's first guests were flown to Maui on a chartered United Airlines DC-8—the first commercial jet to fly straight from the mainland to a neighbor island. It was such a big deal that Maui closed schools so everyone could be at the airport to watch and celebrate. *That's* how much this step meant to Maui, its people, its way of life. The hotel's esteemed first guests included Bob Hope and Bing Crosby (insert *Road to____* joke here) and professional golfer Sam Snead. The latter was essential to showing off the resort's $1+ million golf course designed by our aforementioned buddy, Robert Trent Jones, Sr.

The design of the Sheraton at Ka'anapali was meant to be more than a hotel; it was a Polynesian *experience*. While the Royal Hawaiian on Waikīkī was elegant, it wasn't, ironically, particularly Hawaiian, with its pink façade, Moorish architecture, and colonial furnishings. The Maui Sheraton, on the other hand, featured lava rock columns in the lobby, whaling era décor, hanging gardens, and panoramic ocean views. The designer had a clear sense of what makes Hawai'i special: its natural beauty. He broke down boundaries between the inside and outside, letting it all flow.

I've been in Hawaiian hotels that follow this principle and ones that don't. And the ones that don't—with enclosed hallways and colonial furnishings and plant-free lobbies—make me wonder what the point is of the hotel being in Hawai'i. The St. Regis on Kaua'i (the other upside-down hotel) feels as if it could be on California's Central Coast or in Hong Kong just as easily as Hanalei Bay. It provides elegance and luxury, but misses the mark on the spirit of place. And Hawai'i is a distinct place. It is not interchangeable with Mexico or Jamaica or Mallorca or Rio, or some other locale with sun and palm trees and a sea. Hawai'i has its own culture and history and environment (as do these other places), and I don't want to be cut off from it in my hotel; I prefer to be immersed in it.

On the very rim of Pele's Home,
SHANGRI-LA!
—AD FOR VOLCANO HOUSE, CIRCA 1940S

Before the age of jet travel, visiting the neighbor islands was a schlep and a half. Isabella Bird describes her voyage from Honolulu to Maui as an overnight adventure on the shabby *Kilauea*, a cargo steamer-turned-passenger ship. Her fellow passengers were mostly Hawaiian "men, women, children, dogs, cats, mats, calabashes of poi, cocoanut, bananas, dried figs" and "those odious weak-eyed, pink-nosed Maltese terriers." Giant cockroaches skittered across Bird as she attempted to sleep. The trip from Maui to Hilo on the Big Island of Hawai'i was another overnight passage, this one through vomit-inducing seas. Genteel folks weren't exactly falling all over themselves to make this voyage to the outer islands. Even when propeller planes came on the scene in 1929, it took three hours to fly from Honolulu to Hilo (it now takes fifty minutes), which included a refueling stop on Maui.

Hotels, therefore, weren't in great demand on the neighbor islands. On east Maui, the Wailuku Hotel opened in 1894, and the Grand Hotel in 1916. Over on the west side of the island, the Lāhainā Hotel started welcoming guests in 1901, and not long after was renamed The Pioneer Inn. It's the only hotel of Maui's original three still in existence, now bearing the corporate moniker of Best Western Pioneer Inn. What used to be the Grand in Wailuku is now the site of a Chevron service station, which includes a car wash, a large convenience store, and a restaurant serving everything from pot roast to shoyu chicken to baked 'ōpakapaka (Hawaiian snapper) and hot breakfasts. Hell, if they threw in a few bunk beds, they'd be a full-service hotel owned by locals.

Until the Hilo Hotel opened in 1897, the Big Island's only lodging had been Volcano House, erected about two miles from Halema'uma'u, the summit crater of the island's (still) active volcano, Kīlauea. In the mid-1800s, the hotel was a rustic four-bedroom lodge constructed from a combination of wood and thatch (think a Hawaiian *Little House on the Prairie*). Visitors didn't seem to mind the relative rusticness, though, since getting there from Hilo required a day-long horseback ride with only one brief stop to rest, and anything resembling comfort and warmth was a welcome sight. On her first night at Volcano House in 1873, Isabella Bird watched "the fiery vapours rolling up out of the infinite darkness...The heavy clouds were crimson with the reflection, and soon after midnight jets of flame of a most peculiar colour leapt fitfully into the air, accompanied by a dull throbbing sound."

On our one and only trip to the Big Island in 2007, Michael and I didn't stay at Volcano House (now within the boundaries of Hawai'i Volcanoes National Park), but at Kilauea Lodge. Kilauea Lodge is a former YMCA camp in the fittingly named village of "Volcano," a mile from the park. The Lodge's owners were a former makeup artist on *Magnum, P.I.* (a fact I didn't know at the time, otherwise I would have grilled him for details to pass on to my *Magnum*-obsessed brother) and his wife. A wild feeling inhabited the grounds, with flowers and trees and bamboo spilling into each other. The quaintly decorated rooms were equipped with fireplaces and towel warmers and heavy quilts because—here's a surprising tip—it's cold down there. Or, I should say, *up* there, since Volcano Village is at 3,500 feet.

Complimentary breakfast cooked by the *Magnum* makeup artist himself included either banana French toast with coconut syrup or good ol' eggs and bacon. This was all for $140 a night, about half as much as Volcano House. For these reasons, we've always recommended Kilauea Lodge to friends visiting the Big Island. But as much as we loved it, I still regret that I've never fallen asleep alongside plumes of red smoke and the pulsing earth at Volcano House. That is what the Big Island offers that the others do not: you are an immediate witness to—a participant in—the Earth's geologic past, present and future. You can fall asleep and wake up to it.

Well, it turns out there can be some drawbacks to your hotel sitting near the edge of an active volcano's crater. There's a chance that, say, ninety-six earthquakes in the first ten days of May (as there were in 2018, for instance) will cause major rifts in the volcano, closing most of Hawai'i Volcanoes National Park—including the Volcano House hotel. Under such circumstances, it worked out well that we recommended Kilauea Lodge to our friends Duane and Nancy as they were planning their first trip to the volcano. Which just happened to be for the first week of May 2018.

On May 3, two days before Duane and Nancy were set to leave for their Vacation in Paradise, a 5.1 on the Richter scale earthquake shook southeastern Hawai'i Island. The quake caused new fissures to open up in what's called "the eastern rift zone," which basically means "the eastern area of where the volcano could potentially crack open and create total chaos." And create chaos it did, sending lava flowing down streets and through neighborhoods, consuming everything in its path, including 130 homes. (Within thirty days, that number would leap to six hundred.) The day after the 5.1 quake—the day before Duane and Nancy were set to arrive—forty-five earthquakes of 3.0 or larger rocked the area surrounding the Kīlauea volcano. The biggest was a 6.9 whopper at 12:33 p.m. in the afternoon, destroying the basin floor of the volcano, and sending loads of lava shooting into the air and flowing down its slopes.

This is when Nancy prudently decided to call Kilauea Lodge and find out if, you know, the hotel was still open and not in grave danger of being consumed by molten lava. It was open, and wasn't in any danger, since the new lava flows were about thirty miles away from the town of Volcano. ("I feel that maybe the media didn't do a very good job of explaining where the eruption was actually happening," Nancy told me. Considering that Fox News showed an anchor reporting "Live from the Volcano" and identified the location as "O'ahu"—an entirely different island—I'm inclined to agree).

When Duane and Nancy checked in at Kilauea Lodge, they were told the gas had been shut off because of the aforementioned 6.9 earthquake, and there was not, at the time, hot water in their room. Also, large sections of the adjacent Volcanoes National Park—the area's biggest tourist attraction—were closed. But other than that, the staff downplayed there being any big problem.

The first earthquake our friends felt happened simultaneous to Nancy closing a door in their room, and for a few seconds Duane thought she had slammed the door too hard. Three earthquakes struck between 5:03 and 6:15 p.m. (the first 3.3, and the next two 3.2), so I'm not sure exactly which one caused the Door Slamming Phenomenon. Duane and Nancy proceeded to the Lodge for dinner. At some point, Nancy decided to go browse in the gift shop (I do this too, by the way; I get bored waiting for dinner or waiting for the check, and head out to peruse some little shop). And right then, at 7:06 p.m., a 3.5 earthquake hit.

3.5 might not sound like a very big earthquake—unlike the 6.9, which we can all objectively look at and go "Whoa!" The thing about *this* 3.5 earthquake is its epicenter was pretty much right where Duane and Nancy were staying, and was only 1.3 kilometers from the surface of the earth. I'd never thought about it before, but when Nancy explained that an earthquake closer to the surface shakes you more than one deeper down, it made sense. The rumbling was that much closer to our human bodies and our human possessions. Our human possessions, in this case, included the Lodge's collection of antique beer steins, many of them ceramic, that came flying off the mantle and crashed onto the floor. In the gift shop where Nancy was browsing, dozens of glass curios fell off the shelves and shattered, spewing broken glass everywhere.

Duane's instinct was to grab Nancy and then get the hell outside. That seems like a smart decision, whether it came from the lizard brain or the frontal cortex. When the shaking stopped—both the earth's and their nerves'—they returned to their room and proceeded to remove the wall hangings, most specifically the large picture over the bed. Duane said he wasn't sure they were going to stay there, or if he'd even get a wink of sleep that night. They did end up sleeping, and the next morning decided to roll with it, thinking, "Hey, we're still in Hawai'i."

A couple of days later, a few sections of Hawai'i Volcanoes National Park reopened. Duane and Nancy visited the overlook platform three-quarters of a mile from the Halema'uma'u crater. This view basically looks like the surface of some barren planet, flat and mostly a greyish black with plumes of smoke rising up from the crater. The plumes of smoke are small enough to just make you go, "That's so cool!" and not "Holy shit, run for your lives." So

Nancy and Duane were staring at said plumes and had hit the "I'm kind of bored/should we take off?" phase, when they suddenly heard a tremendous rumbling that, interestingly, did not rock the ground they were standing on. The lava lake of Halemaʻumaʻu crater had just *dropped* 720 feet. The sudden collapse caused pieces of the crater wall to fall into the lava lake and explode, creating a gigantic plume of smoke and ash resembling the Kuwaiti oil fires from 1991. It was such a rare event that even the park rangers on site were excited, Duane and Nancy said.

"How did you feel, getting to witness an event like that?" I asked them.

"I felt privileged," Duane said. "Well, maybe privileged is not the right word, but I felt special. I felt lucky." But isn't that—lucky—the essence of privilege?

There's a great parallel between the Hawaiian culture and the Disney culture.
—WEBSITE COPY FOR AULANI, A DISNEY RESORT & SPA

I'm a sucker for brand loyalty. More specifically, I'm a sucker for typing my frequent flier/guest number into a reservation form and earning points and perks. This is how Michael and I ended up at the Hilton Waikoloa Village after we left the volcano. On the Big Island's sunny northwest Kona Coast, the Hilton Waikoloa Village was much more affordable than the Fairmont Orchid or the Mauna Kea (the latter built by Laurance S. Rockefeller), while still being away from the "hustle and bustle" of the town of Kailua-Kona. This is ridiculously relative, by the way: with a population of almost twelve thousand, the town is still small by mainland standards. Considering we were used to Kōloa on Kaua'i—with a population of not quite two thousand—we assumed Kailua-Kona would be too busy for our tastes. And, apparently, we hadn't learned our lesson from Waikīkī: that any Hilton with the word "village" in its name meant "over the top."

From an aerial view, the Hilton Waikoloa probably looks like any other Hawaiian resort: lush, landscaped grounds, sprawling buildings, and an elaborate, meandering pool fronting the ocean. When you zoom in a little closer, though, you see the ways this hotel took the Polynesian playground at least one step too far and burst into the realm of Disneyfication. The property is vast—sixty-two acres—and the most efficient way to traverse it is by one of their "Swiss-made, air-conditioned trams." I'm not sure why it matters that they're Swiss made, but the hotel makes sure to highlight this feature on its webpage. When you board the tram from the lobby, you're also boarding with babies, toddlers, tweens and teens, their parents and grandparents, strollers, shopping bags, backpacks, and lots of "Whew, it's been a hot and busy day" exhaustion. This makes your fellow riders neither particularly friendly nor cheery.

The hotel's 1,243 rooms are divided among three towers. Each tower is its own ecosystem, with shops, restaurants, a concierge, and birds, birds, birds. We were originally lodged in the Lagoon Tower, next to the main pool. The

Lagoon Tower surrounds a huge tropical atrium that seems perfectly lovely until around sunset, when over a hundred myna birds start squawking loudly. (One TripAdvisor reviewer described them as "about 12 million myna birds," giving you a sense of how vociferous they are.) This cacophony continues for a few hours, goes quiet, then starts up again in the early morning hours. It's also possible—based on descriptions in other reviews—that the noise actually continues throughout the night, and I just passed out from sheer exhaustion for a few hours before reawakening to the Hitchcockian nightmare.

We asked to be moved to a quieter room. Our new home in the Ocean Tower also abutted an atrium filled with myna birds that could be heard dusk to dawn. They weren't quite as loud as our previous location (I assume this means there were only *six* million), and a pillow over my head muffled them enough to get some sleep. Who were these other guests, I wonder, for whom sleep deprivation is no biggie? Sure, some folks slumber so hard they wouldn't be roused if the volcano burst in a Vesuvius-like eruption. But for many, I suspect, the rest of their vacation experience—swimming with dolphins and puttering around in mahogany boats and drinking in papaya sunsets while watching a gigantic lūʻau—was so enjoyable that the lack of sleep wasn't only worth the experience, but was actually part of the exoticism. Perhaps the myna birds were as exotic to them as the guttural call of Belize's howler monkeys had been to us in a jungle hotel the previous year. Hearing the tropical squawk while lying on crisp white sheets and down pillows allows a tourist to feel adventurous while still being pleasantly coddled.

The Ocean Tower sits at the opposite end of the tram line from the Lagoon Tower. The tram ride to the lobby took ten to fifteen minutes, not including the ten-minute wait for the tram to arrive. The lagoon's "magical mahogany boats" (I'm surprised the hotel didn't put a ™ after that) were also available to ferry us around, but they were slower and ran on a less frequent schedule, so they were more for the scenic route than efficiency. The walk from our room to the lobby traversed about a mile, part of which passed by interesting bronze and gold-leaf Asian art. But if we wanted to be trapped inside a dim corridor, we would have stayed in rainy Portland. Regardless of transportation method, running back to our room to retrieve sunscreen or a hat or a book could take forty minutes round-trip, and more often resulted in us waving the white flag—either forgoing the forgotten item, or just collapsing in our room and calling it a day.

We had clearly made some tactical errors when booking this hotel, and one was not understanding how far it is from the ("bustling") town of Kailua-Kona, a place where kamaʻāina actually live. I don't think we'd yet figured out how much that meant to us. How much we didn't want to stay trapped in a resort experience, how detached from Hawai'i that made us feel. We also didn't understand how truly *big* the Big Island is (I know, duh), and therefore how spread apart everything is. Kailua-Kona was forty minutes away, which wasn't super convenient for just zipping over for dinner. The closest dining option outside the hotel was the Kings' Shops, a white-stuccoed open-air mall with nearly identical siblings in every planned resort in the Islands. The Kings' Shops complex is bigger than most of its kin, with a Macy's and nowhere near enough parking. We discovered this when attempting to procure dinner on Saturday night. It was like Christmas season at the Mall of America: drivers (us) stalking people back to their cars in hopes of claiming their parking space, only to be cut off by another driver (the enemy). We ultimately retreated to the hotel in defeat.

The hotel offers a shuttle bus to the Kings' Shops, and the first time we tried to take it was also the last. The usual shuttle stop in front of the hotel was closed, so we were diverted downstairs into the 1.4-mile tunnel system the staff uses to eat meals, change into their uniforms, sort recycling, do laundry, and move around the grounds without clogging up the aboveground arteries. Fluorescent lights illuminate the concrete tunnels that employees are relegated to. There were no palm trees, no trade winds, no ocean views, and no sunlight. Nowhere have I seen a starker contrast between the fantasy paradise constructed for guests and the reality lived by workers. We waited for the shuttle in this limbo between worlds for twenty minutes, but it never showed.

The only time we actually made it to the Kings' Shops was when we walked, which seems like the obvious solution all along, since it's only a mile from the front of the hotel—but keep in mind the amount of effort it took to simply get from our room to the lobby. It required forethought as well as a bit of physical endurance. By the time we actually made it to the Kings' Shops, we were so shell-shocked by resort prices that we opted for Subway sandwiches while watching a small hula show.

There was a lot of giving up required on this visit—how much sleep we got, what and where we ate, how we moved about the grounds, what was convenient to do. This is not an accident. The resort—like the prototype in Ka'anapali—is built to keep people from leaving it. That's how they make back the hundreds of millions of dollars it costs to build and operate such an elaborate system. They don't want guests to spend their money in local towns and off-the-beaten-path restaurants. They don't want you to visit the island's natural attractions unless *their* concierge, or one of *their* tour operators gets a commission for it. The hotel, at every step, manufactures and controls your experience of what Hawai'i is, and what it will mean to you.

Not all travelers agree that my experiences are problems. On just about every review website, the Hilton Waikoloa consistently rates four out of five stars. The constant swirl of activity is perfect for children and extroverts and visitors who are mostly looking for a sunny vacation, and it doesn't matter if it's in Hawai'i or Florida or Mazatlán. And for those who aren't thrilled with the staged atmosphere, maybe the ocean views and warm breezes and palm trees and sunsets turned sanguine by volcano ash and smoke transcend the manufactured version of paradise. Maybe, even still, the true essence of Hawai'i comes through.

But to me, this hotel seemed prouder of the fact that your kids can spend a half hour swimming with dolphins for $210 than it was of any aspect of Hawaiian heritage. I don't know if it's because of this weird sanitization, or because on any given day there are three thousand guests, but the employees didn't seem particularly happy to be there. They didn't smile or make conversation. I suspect there's a negative feedback loop at work. The kind of guests who don't care if their hotel represents any aspect of Hawai'i might not care much about the people who live in Hawai'i. Every interaction we witnessed between guests and employees was that of someone expecting to be served because they paid X amount of dollars, and the person who served them—not because they enjoyed meeting people from all over the world, but because they had to pay rent. One attitude continually begets the next, and the cycle of colonialism continues uninterrupted.

Discover the true spirit of Hawaii around every turn
—Website for Grand Hyatt Kauai Resort and Spa

Blue sky arcs overhead, sun-shaped marble tiles lie beneath my feet, and plumeria-scented air surrounds. An old Hawaiian woman named Auntie Janet teaches 'ukulele to two girls and their mothers on rattan sofas. A red hyacinth macaw named Nīele and a blue macaw named Duke periodically squawk like fire alarms. All around me are ruffled fan palms, birds of paradise, dendrobium orchids, firecracker-red ginger, philodendrons, fiddlehead ferns, purple ti plants, and at least two dozen bushes and flowers I can't identify. I am inside and I am outside all at the same time. I am in paradise, my expectation of a Hawaiian vacation met. I'm in the lobby of the Grand Hyatt on Kaua'i.

The hotel opened in Po'ipū in November 1990 as a Hyatt Regency. By that time, developers had observed nearly a century of what worked and what didn't in a Hawaiian resort. The Hilton Waikoloa Village (originally also a Hyatt) had only been open for a few years when development of the Po'ipū hotel got underway, but planners already realized, "Whoa, this fantasy resort concept has gotten *waaay* out of hand. We need to reel. It. Back. In." They were convinced that the spirit of place needed to be not just a part of the resort experience, but actually needed to BE the resort experience. It would require a major economic gamble, though. Even though the Hyatt was planned on fifty acres—only twelve less than the Waikoloa Village resort—it would have *half* the number of rooms. Half the occupancy would mean half the income…unless they charged twice as much. But what could they offer to justify such a price? They could offer a Polynesian paradise.

First of all, there are no towers. None of the Grand Hyatt's sprawling buildings are higher than a mature coconut palm, which, in this case, equals four stories. White stucco walls, green tiled roofs, and spacious lānais evoke an early twentieth-century plantation vibe (an aesthetic possibly more pleasant to the descendants of people not required to work on said plantations). Almost all the common spaces, including hallways, are open-air, with gentle trade winds and flora perfume sweeping through. Lobby décor includes a wooden poi-pounding board, sculptures of men paddling outrigger canoes, and two really tall (like, at least twenty feet) kāhili. Kāhili are traditional ceremonial poles topped with Dr. Seuss-like mounds of feathers. The feathers on the Grand Hyatt's kāhili are black. The concierge told me she didn't remember what kind of bird they came from, but said, "I think it's now extinct." Kāhili were featured in ancient royal ceremonies, and the bigger the pole, the more powerful the ali'i. In the Grand Hyatt they're perched behind the Avis Rental Car desk, an apt metaphor for the supremacy of tourism in Hawai'i.

There are no trams, or boats, or any form of intra-resort transportation other than walking. Sandstone paths wind along the lava-lined oceanfront, over a lagoon filled with mandarin koi and black swans, past several cascading waterfalls, and through lushly planted gardens. It all blends together so perfectly that you don't notice how perfect it is unless you stop and think, "Wait, how did a human being plan this?" Then it seems impossible. Divine, even.

There's only been one time when the distance from our room at the Hyatt to the idyllic lobby or meandering pool seemed exhausting, and it was just enough to fog my paradisiacal goggles. We were placed in a wing we didn't even know existed, in what we'd call a daylight basement in a residential house. The lānai opened to a sparkling view of the ocean, but our roof was a lawn that people walked on. The hallway outside our door was underground and had a "place that time forgot" vibe. Not only was it dark (and smelled like laundry detergent), but it was as if the decoration budget had run out down there. In other wings, shiny koa side tables sat between doors, with a mirror or artwork hanging above them. The table outside our door was like a first-apartment basic from Ikea, with no décor to be found.

The walk to the lobby (and the pool and the beach) was not only long, but circuitous. From our room, we'd walk down a dark interior hallway, then take a right, walk down another long dark interior hallway, then make a right, a left, and another left to an elevator. The elevator took us to the fourth floor, where we hung left, walked down a hallway that at least opened to the outside, then took a right and GLORY BE we were finally in the lobby, the spot of the aforementioned marble-tiled sun.

We tried to find shortcuts. Strolling the outdoor path at least gave us an ocean view, but involved crossing two or three bridges and hiking uphill, and wasn't any more efficient or less confusing. The quickest route we discovered involved exiting our floor from what looked like a service entrance. Seriously: it's dirty and unmarked, with no path leading to or from it, and for sure looked like you shouldn't go in there without a machete and a hoe. But if we exited that door and trekked across the lawn to a path, then walked around the hotel to another path that took us past the backside of the spa, and then the front side of the spa, it delivered us to the lobby the fastest. We didn't discover this until after I'd called the front desk and requested a room closer in, above ground. But my *long and circuitous* point is that, from our original room, the resort seemed too big, too sprawling, and not very user-friendly—just like the Hilton Waikoloa.

The irony is it was also the most expensive room we'd ever booked at the Grand Hyatt. I'd paid for the room in advance during an uncharacteristic spending spree that we now call "The Year of Spending Dangerously." And guess what? It turns out the more you pay, the fewer imperfections you're inclined to let slide. My expectations of "paradise" were elevated. If this had been our first visit, we might not have made another. We'd say, "We're paying *how* much for this?" which, in fact, is exactly what I said when I asked to be moved. I said a lot of things that reeked of entitlement, like, "We're return guests," and "I'm a Platinum member," and "I paid with my Hyatt Visa card." I also said, "I have chronic fatigue syndrome," then felt as if I needed to walk around looking fatigued for the rest of our stay, in case anyone doubted me.

Here's what I didn't say, because it's difficult to fit into a phone call or tweet: this hotel matters to me more than is normal for a hotel to matter to a person. We spent three days here on our honeymoon, six months after my mom died, and it's when and where I fell in love with Kaua'i. The next time we came was in 2000, after Michael closed his CD store and our dog died. Michael was mourning his lifelong dream to run his own music shop, and we were both mourning our sweetest, goofiest best friend-baby. We came to the hotel after I lost thirty pounds and got in shape. I'd planned to reward myself with a trip to Canyon Ranch in Tucson, but when we looked at the *holy crap* prices, we realized we could actually afford to go to Kaua'i for the same.

We stayed at the hotel after my dad was in rehab for Ambien abuse. We stayed there when my brother first became extremely ill and disabled. When my dad tried to commit suicide three times in three months and was put in the psych ward, we couldn't afford to stay at the hotel, but Michael booked us an affordable condo next door. We walked around the Hyatt's verdant grounds and lay in a hammock together and treated ourselves to a fish dinner at the hotel's fancy restaurant. We went to the hotel after my dad died, and then after my brother died the following year and I was bereft and alone. We could never afford to stay there for an entire week, so we'd book five nights at a cheaper condo, and then use points for two or three nights at the hotel. Kauaʻi was the place where my soul belonged, and this hotel had saved my life again and again…but this seemed like an insane speech to deliver to a front desk clerk or a concierge, so I said what I said, and what they most likely heard was: I am an entitled tourist, and I deserve better than that what I've been given.

Wailea's First Resort is Now Its Newest

We invite you to tap into the energy and spirit of a place, and an island, like no other.

—WEBSITE FOR THE WAILEA BEACH RESORT—MARRIOTT, MAUI

It took me twenty-three years to return to the Inter-Continental on Maui, the home-away-from home for my dad and brother and I during the eighties. I knew that south Maui wouldn't much resemble the stomping grounds of my youth. Outlet stores and upscale shopping centers and strip malls proliferated throughout Kīhei and Wailea. More hotels and condos sprang up on what used to be tangles of wild kiawe and fountain grass. I knew the InterContinental wouldn't be the same; for that matter, it wasn't even called the InterContinental anymore. In the 1990s it was bought by Aston Hotels & Resorts, and then Outrigger Hotels and Resorts, but neither was particularly committed to bringing the resort up to modern standards. Travel writers described the property as drab, dark, frayed, and stained. My family's treasured terrain had become a cheaper compromise amid resort gems, tourmaline set among rubies, sapphires, and diamonds.

It wasn't until Marriott bought the hotel that anyone thought investing money might beget more money. In 2008, they unveiled a $60 million renovation along with a mouthful of a name change: the Wailea Marriott Beach Resort and Spa. Beige carpet was ripped out of guest rooms and replaced with white tile off of which sand could be easily swept. The orange and green floral bedspreads gave way to white damask duvets and that confusing double-sheeting that makes it impossible to throw back just one layer if you get too hot. An adults-only "Serenity Pool" was installed on what had previously been a vast lawn reaching towards the sea. The Inu Inu bar was replaced by a day spa and workout room, and the Liberty House clothing store was part of the new conference center—gone not just from the hotel, but from all of Hawai'i, having been absorbed by Macy's.

Apparently, that still wasn't enough to keep pace with the island's other resorts, so eight years later the hotel underwent another renovation, this one clocking in at $100 million. My 2017 return to Maui was four months after it had been "unveiled." (I mean, really. It's a 22-acre piece of land, not the car of the future hidden behind a velvet curtain. Can they find a more accurate verb?) They changed the name again, this time to the Wailea Beach Resort—Marriott, Maui (why or how this is better than the previous name is entirely baffling). The Lanai Terrace/ aka: the coffee shop was now called Humble Market Kitchin [sic, that's really how it's spelled], part of Roy Yamaguchi's Pacific Rim culinary empire, and it didn't serve club sandwiches or shrimp Louis salads, but $22 ramen and $43 fish. The Kiawe Broiler was transformed into KAPA Bar & Grill, where a hot dog goes for $17. What was once the Luau Pool's lawn—where my brother and our friends and I swam and played volleyball—was now a gigantic aquatic playground with four water slides and an "interactive splash zone, with water guns, spraying sea mammal sculptures and bubblers." (Are the water guns spraying sea mammal sculptures? Are the sea mammal sculptures spraying something—we hope water? If there ever was a need for an Oxford comma, it's between the words "sea mammal sculptures" and "bubblers.")

They built bigger pools and better restaurants and spiffed up the guest rooms, and bragged about it a *lot*. But this newest renovation was irrelevant to me. The hotel wasn't going to look like where we'd stayed in the eighties, and removing one extra layer of familiarity made no difference. I also believed that no matter how many new pools were built or how the hotel's cosmetics and accessories had changed, there would be something familiar about this place where my dad and brother and I had sown roots. The essence of what we fell in love with would be imbedded in the lava rock shore. The spirit of my family would hang in the sweet, moist air.

When I pulled my car into the porte-cochère, not sure where to park because the parking lot wasn't where it used to be, I saw the lobby was totally different—but somehow the same—and got dizzy. The unsteadiness didn't reside in my head so much as my body, and I almost tipped over when getting out of the car. Employees in aloha shirts mingled in a small group, constituting some sort of reception team. They greeted me cheerfully and I spilled out, "Check in?"

A young local named Deanna said, "I can do that! Come with me."

We rounded the corner, and she went into a recessed booth. It used to be a bar, that space, where people could grab a cocktail while walking through the lobby. The last time I'd been there, for my honeymoon, Miles the bartender was trapped in the cubicle. I'd first ordered Diet Cokes and virgin daiquiris from him at the Luau Pool when I was fourteen. I felt so grown-up introducing him to my husband and drinking his trademark banana javas (see appendix for recipe).

Behind me and Deanna was the open-air, square, covered lobby where I used to sit and write in my journal. It's also where I'd wait for John, the cute room service waiter to walk by. John was always ferrying food, which was the perfect excuse to not have to stand and talk to me (aka:

awkward teenage tourist) for more than a couple of minutes. "I better get going before this melts," he'd say about the banana split in a glass goblet he was carrying.

My post for stalking John was now an ultra-modern chill lounge with low-backed banquet booths, long tables, and a rectangular aquarium filled with koi. Jawaiian music played overhead, and trade winds rustled palm trees. The afternoon sun bounced off the crests of waves, lighting the west Maui mountains with a theatrical glow.

"Wow, this is an amazing view," I said.

"My office!" Deanna said. Resort employees—by the pool, in the lobby, on the beach—use this phrase often.

"I used to come here all the time in the eighties when this was the InterContinental, so this is kinda of trippy," I said. "I'm pretty discombobulated."

"Oh, it's so different now," she said. "We just had this huge renovation."

I thought about that word—renovation—and what it means: fixed up, changed, beautified, modernized. If this place, where my dad and brother and I spent time together as a family, where I did so much of my coming of age, hadn't so much disappeared as it had been *renovated*, then maybe that was true for my family, too. Maybe they weren't really gone, maybe they were just…the whole metaphor fell apart immediately. The reason my dad and brother are dead is precisely because they were unfixable, resistant to change, unwilling to be repaired and restored.

The hotel's renovation rendered it virtually unrecognizable to me. It stirred almost no nostalgia, conjured up no forgotten memories. I stood in front of the rooms Steve and my dad and I stayed in—6410 and 6412. I could locate them with my eyes closed. I could locate them stoned from weed I bought from Miles, dazed by too many hours in the fierce sun, drunk from rum procured at a bar that didn't card me, floating from being kissed by a blond, blue-eyed surfer five years older than I was. I stood in front of the doors and faced out towards what I'd seen every time I left my room: a grove of majesty palms. I took a picture of the trees, then turned to take a picture of the doors, *our* doors, and noticed the room numbers: 4610 and 4612.

The cognitive dissonance looped me for a moment. I know that memory is unreliable, and we often crystalize untrue information and believe it to be fact. But I knew, still know, without a single doubt, that 6410 and 6412 were our room numbers in the eighties. I even knew why the rooms were numbered such: they were in building six, on the fourth floor, the tenth and twelfth rooms down from where the hallway started, from the elevator where I'd been kissed by the blond surfer. I consulted the current map for the Marriott. The building I was standing in was now called building four. But there was no explanation for why 6 would be the next digit in the room numbers. It was still the fourth floor—they hadn't somehow lifted the entire hotel up two stories. Somewhere in all the improvements and renovations and additions, a seemingly arbitrary choice was made to change the building numbers. Because all change is good, and all change has to be absolute. Shops and restaurants and old hotels throughout the state were demolished for bigger, better, newer ones. Beaches and kiawe and cane fields were plowed over to make way for aquariums and malls. Residents got priced out of the towns in which they worked—all in the name of progress. All in the name of money.

Job Summary

Wash, mop, and clean the pool deck. Obtain, fold, and stack towels according to company procedures. Reach overhead and below the knees, including bending, twisting, pulling, and stooping.

—Job description for a Pool & Beach Attendant, Sheraton Princess, Honolulu

---

Joan Didion said that "great hotels have always been social ideas, flawless mirrors to the particular societies they service." Who is the society a hotel services? On the surface, their guests, of course. But when the hospitality industry is the bedrock of a community's economy, their purpose is not just to serve guests, but also to provide jobs. In theory, the goal of providing jobs is giving people a means of supporting themselves. But in Hawai'i, 7 percent of residents employed in accommodations and 31.8 percent in the food and beverage industries live below the poverty line. Those above poverty line but *under* "self-sufficiency income" are 25.3 percent in accommodations and 38.4 percent in food & beverage. I'm going to make a bold proclamation here and suggest the hotel industry is not doing a great job of serving Hawai'i's residents.

And what of Native Hawaiians, the people whose land was taken away in order to build these hotels? What are their roles in the industry, especially in the better-paying management positions? I sent emails to the PR folks at Hilton Waikoloa Village, the Hilton Hawaiian Village on Waikīkī, and the Royal Hawaiian Hotel asking what percentage of their management positions (lower, middle, and upper) were held by Native Hawaiians. The Royal Hawaiian didn't respond to my request, and the Hilton Hawaiian Village said, "The resort would like to pass on this opportunity to be featured" (Um, they do understand I'll still write about them, right?). The Hilton Waikoloa Village asked me to explain "in what nature the information you're requesting will be included." I clarified that I'm interested in the evolution of the Hawaiian resort and its place in the culture (while avoiding incendiary words like "colonialism" and "imperialism"), and then I never heard back. I understand that I don't possess high-level press credentials or anything else that would make these PR reps take me seriously. My writing is of little importance to them. That being said, if an equitable percentage of management positions were held by Native Hawaiians, that's a fact the hotels would want to highlight. Almost every major business on the mainland has calculated the percentage of African-American and Latinx employees at all levels. It's that important to show their "commitment to diversity." So these hotels are either not keeping track of how many Native Hawaiians they employ in white-collar jobs, or they *are* keeping track and don't want that number exposed.

Consulting with the US Bureau of Labor Statistics didn't help much, since they only provide stats for Native Hawaiians in management positions in the entire tourism sector, not just accommodations and food. (Technically, "tourism" is not an industry classification unto itself, but consists of a variety of sectors such as transportation, cleaning and maintenance, architecture and engineering, construction, entertainment, etc., in addition to jobs specific to hotels and restaurants.) In the entire tourism sector, Native Hawaiians (including hapa) account for only 12.9 percent of management positions—while comprising 26 percent of the total population—and earn less than their non-Hawaiian counterparts.

This is a whole lot of numbers, of percentages of this and that, that primarily add up to indicating that the hotel industry doesn't have a commitment to support the society in which they exist. They do offer jobs, but at low wages, despite the fact that their very existence—their vast consumption of resources—is a significant factor in jacking up the cost of living in Hawai'i. Back in the plantation days, owners provided their low-wage workers with housing and food. The living conditions were usually pretty shitty, so it's not as if I'm advocating for that level of serfdom. And since most of Hawai'i's planned resort communities have already been, err, *planned* and built, it's too late to fold in the idea of affordable housing for the workforce. One of the reasons new affordable housing is hard to build is because land is so expensive, and the reason the land is so expensive is because hotel and condo developers drove up prices in the areas where residents work. It's a circle so vicious that it deserves a canto in Dante's *Inferno*.

Returning to Didion's idea, we can only conclude that the society that Hawaiian resorts serve are guests with disposable income. Like me. My degree of disposable income has differed over the decades, from scrimping and taking money out of savings and eating at happy hour in bars, to being able to stay in nice resorts twice in one year and enjoying three-course dinners. But even when it was a scrimp-and-save situation, there's no denying I was still coming from a place of privilege. My very relationship with the Islands—solidified when my dad, a white mainlander, was building on Maui—is predicated on privilege. While other people might view Hawai'i as a once-in-a-lifetime trip, a "Wow, I hope I get to go there someday" idea, I view it as a necessity, a lifeline.

But not as a right.

I now keep that in mind whenever I visit: it is not my right to use and abuse the 'āina and the kama'āina. Yes, these resorts were built for me and my ilk, and yes, without tourism the Hawaiian economy would collapse. But this is because of my country's colonialism, imperialism, violence, war. It is not a favor that I am doing for anyone but myself. And maybe keeping all that in mind while on vacation sounds like a *bummer*, but it operates as just the opposite for me. It fills me with a sense of gratitude, of honor, of respect and love. Dare I even say—dare I appropriate this word?—it fills me with aloha.

Da Kine | Honu

A HONU IS A HAWAIIAN GREEN SEA TURTLE, OR THE *chelonia mydas*, if you're into thinking of things that way. They've been around for two hundred million years, and are protected as an endangered species. It's strange, really: for the first forty-five years of my life, I didn't find honu particularly beautiful or special or cool. I never understood why people had pictures of them on T-shirts and coffee mugs and jewelry. But six months after my brother died, we were staying at a townhouse near a shore where honu swam. My mind was a constant whir of *my whole family is dead. Steve never knew I loved him. He was in such pain. Did my dad kill himself? I'll never see my childhood home again. I almost landed in a mental hospital. This whole world is unknown to me.*

On languid afternoons, Michael and I would stroll to the shore and watch the honu ride waves toward the lava tide pools. The swells crashed against the shore with violent intensity, but the honu always emerged unscathed. Their flippers were stronger than the waves. Their shells harder than the rocks. "There!" Michael would point when a honu popped up its leathered head to breathe and absorb the sun. Then it dove back down, munched on some algae, and swam back out into the watery expanse with enviable power and grace.

When I sat and watched the honu, the whir stopped. The only sounds in my head were the wind and the

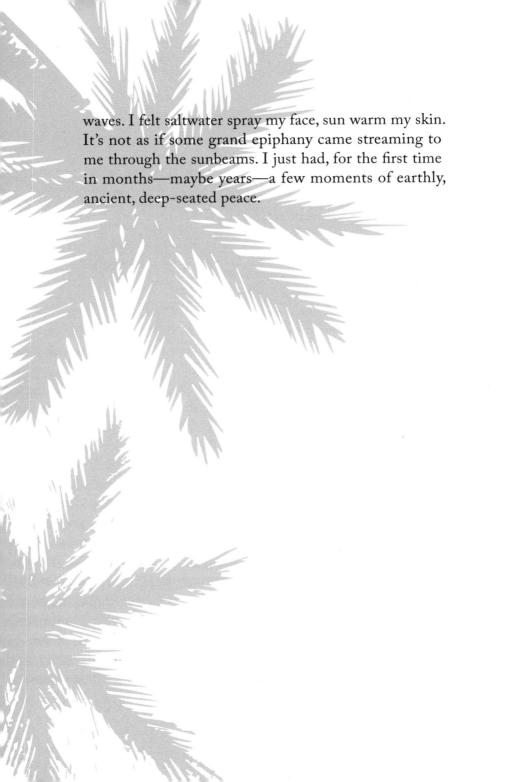

waves. I felt saltwater spray my face, sun warm my skin. It's not as if some grand epiphany came streaming to me through the sunbeams. I just had, for the first time in months—maybe years—a few moments of earthly, ancient, deep-seated peace.

Hōʻihi: The Meaning of Respect

LACK OF RESPECT IS UNEQUIVOCALLY THE MOST FRE-quent complaint levied against tourists in Hawaiʻi. No respect for the land, the people, the wildlife, the culture. "Okay, but what does that mean, exactly?" a client recently asked me. "To show respect?" I was sort of gobsmacked. I'd been going around parroting this phrase, but wasn't able to come up with a quick—or easy—answer to this very obvious question.

It may seem pedantic, but etymology—roots—is often a helpful place to turn when we're trying to unpack meaning. The Hawaiian word for respect is hōʻihi, which breaks down as: hō = to give or to show, and ʻihi = sacred, dignified. Hōʻihi means to give dignity to someone or something, to treat it as sacred. There's a reciprocity inherent in that definition; treating some-one with dignity also shows that *you* are dignified. In English, the word "respect" is derived from Latin and literally translates as "to look back," and was generally thought to mean "to regard, to consider." The implica-tion is that if you give someone more than a passing glance, if you truly consider them, you will have deeper regard for them.

Somewhere around the 1580s, the word transmuted into meaning a "feeling of esteem excited by actions or attributes of someone or something; courteous or considerate treatment due to *personal worth or power*." That whole business about "regarding and considering" somehow took a back seat. Listen, I'm not saying that every mainland Joe and Josie Blow is attuned to the modern etymology of "respect" and applies it accordingly. But that meaning, one of power and worth, is deeply woven into our cultural understanding of who deserves respect. And based on that cultural understanding, we would not be inclined to show respect to, for instance: a rock. A gecko. A ti leaf. A person who does not own land. Or speak pristine American English. Or work indoors. Or drive a rust-free car. But in Hawai'i? Well, the land, the 'āina, is sacred, and the people of Hawai'i are all children of the land. So everyone deserves respect.

But it turns out "show respect" is one of those phrases that *sounds* self-explanatory in the same way "don't be an asshole" should be, but actually requires some parsing. Especially in Hawai'i, where visitors have flown a long way and paid a lot of money for a dream vacation in paradise. So, I'm going to break it down the best I can, in five examples. And despite the supposed effectiveness of positive reinforcement, it's easier to illustrate using examples of what not to do.

1. One day my friend Lauren, who lives on Maui, was on the beach meditating—sitting still, eyes closed—when a woman interrupted her to ask where the

turtles are. Lauren opened her eyes and told the woman that you had to swim out to that reef (pointing) to see the honu. The woman was visibly and audibly annoyed. "But I was told my kids could see them from the beach," she complained. Lauren said, "No, they're out there." The woman said, "Fine! I'll just go to another beach then." (Can you imagine how *disappointed* Lauren must have been that this woman decamped for another beach?)

This anecdote illuminated a fact I'd never quite grasped before in such an obvious way: the people of Hawai'i are not there to be our tour guides, especially when they're not, you know, working as tour guides. Their private time and private space is just that: private. It belongs to them, not tourists. So, like, a couple of years ago when I asked the local guy who was spearfishing what that thing attached to the ass of his diving outfit was, and he replied crustily "Octopus," and I said, "Wow, that's cool!" and he turned away from me *rudely* (as I took a picture of his octopus-adorned ass), it's because he was doing his own thing—possibly his job—and wasn't there to provide trivia or entertainment for tourists.

On the mainland, we can usually assess whether someone is open to engaging in conversation. Do they have headphones on? Do they look you in the eye? Do they smile or frown? Do they have their eyes closed while sitting quietly by themselves? Are they scrambling among lava rocks with a spear in one hand and a bag of fish over their shoulder, etc.? We can and should apply the same criteria to folks in Hawai'i.

The other incredibly-obvious-I-hope issue in this vignette is how annoyed the woman was that the honu weren't right where she wanted them to be, convenient for her and her children. I fear that tourists have become so accustomed to aquariums and zoos and hotels that show off honu and dolphins and other slightly exotic animals, that we forget they are *wild-life*. These animals don't exist to entertain us. They have their own deeply imbedded reasons for being where they are, and for doing whatever they're doing. Of course, human history is awash with examples of humans using animals for our own purposes. We either hunt them into extinction or near-extinction (whales, turtles, seals, etc.) or we simply don't care about the collateral damage our "growth" and "progress" causes hundreds of species of birds, fish, bugs, bats and other creatures. We, humans, are what made Hawai'i home to nearly one quarter of the United States' endangered species of animals, marine mammals, and birds. We should be grateful those honu are anywhere on this earth, even if they are out of our own sight.

2. A couple of years ago, my friend Michelle and I were sitting on Wailea Beach when we noticed a crowd of people in the shallow water, slowly moving together in a circle. They were pointing their cameras and snorkel masks down. That's when I realized they'd encircled a honu who'd swam close to shore. As it tried to swim away, they moved with and *around* it, essentially keeping the honu trapped. One guy in the bunch with a

loud Brooklyn accent told everyone to give it space, but they paid no heed. I looked behind me, hoping someone with authority would tell them to stop. Two local guys who set up beach chairs and umbrellas for the nearby hotel watched, bored.

Building on the idea that the Hawaiian wildlife is not there simply to entertain us, I'd also like to point out that it's *illegal* to harass a honu, an endangered species, and that includes impeding its movement. One of the current threats to honu survival is a disease called fibropapillomatosis. Tumors with a cauliflower-like appearance grow on the turtles' torsos (outside and in), impeding their ability to see, eat, swim, and, therefore, live. While scientists haven't been able to pinpoint exactly why turtles contract the virus, strong links have been made to environmental pollution, and *stress*. You know, like being caged in by human bodies and unable to swim free.

When I relayed this story to Lauren, she asked if I told the tourists to back the fuck away from the honu. I didn't, because I suspected I didn't have enough agency for anyone to listen to me. I was just a tourist, like them, after all. Who did I think I was? But I have felt badly about that ever since, knowing that by passively witnessing this abuse, I was no better than the perpetrators. I also suspect that the local guys behind me didn't intervene because they'd learned tourists paying $500+ a night to stay in a resort don't like being told what to do—especially by young brown men making minimum wage. So for the love of hōʻihi, don't mess with the wildlife. Let them be what they are. Wild.

3. And now for an example that encapsulates the previous two: A small crowd gathered around a roped-off perimeter to view a three-year-old monk seal who'd come ashore on Poʻipū Beach. Volunteers from the Kauaʻi Monk Seal Watch posted their usual signage telling people not to disturb the seal (don't use flash photography, don't yell, and for the love of god, don't touch it). Beachgoers gathered because the seal was super cute, and anything we're told to stay away from is something we naturally want to know more about. Most of the time, monk seals just sleep when they come ashore, but every once in a while they roll over slowly or scratch their head with a front flipper (this is exactly as adorable as it sounds). Spectators get super excited while trying not to make a lot of noise (my reaction is always to grab Michael's arm and quietly squeal, "Honey!").

This particular morning, a volunteer stood on one side of the perimeter talking to an onlooker about the seal. On the far other side of the perimeter—a good 150 feet away—a middle-aged white guy yelled *across the seal*, "Sir! Will you move to the side? You're in my picture. Sir!" (I guess he thought "Sir" made his yelling polite?)

The volunteer was doing his job (unpaid, yes, but an important job nonetheless). He was there to make sure tourists didn't cause stress or harm to the very creature the yelling guy was so anxious to capture a picture of. Let's not even start on whether Yelling Guy has ever heard of cropping a picture or using Photoshop. Let's just focus on the fact that the volunteer is 100 percent part of the experience of seeing a monk seal come ashore. The volunteer was there because monk seals are endangered. Around 1,100 to 1,400 live in the entire archipelago: 900-ish in the reefs, islets, and atolls that make up the unpopulated Northwestern Hawaiian Islands (NWHI), and 150 to 300 in the main islands. That's *it* in the entire world. While their population in the main Hawaiian Islands is slowly growing, they are declining in the NWHI at a rate of about 4 percent per year, constituting a net die-off.

These poor monk seals have it rough. Humans hunted them into near extinction in the 1800 and 1900s, and then we built on the beaches and shorelines the seals need for molting and nursing their pups, and we continue to pump pollution into their home waters. And in case human dumbassery isn't enough, sharks and aggressive male monk seals attack and kill young monk seals and females. It's as if everything in their environment is conspiring to kill them off. But, to our credit, human intervention—organizations like the National Oceanic and Atmospheric Administration and Kaua'i Monk Seal Watch—has actually made them *less* endangered. They'd be declining at an even greater rate without these efforts. So, if you're not willing to have that volunteer in your picture, perhaps you're more attached to the *idea* of Hawaiian sea life than the reality of it: that these cute, cool creatures need to be protected. From us.

4. Just because someone is doing their job doesn't mean you're entitled to act...well, entitled. Like they're your servant. This Rule of Respect runs close to basic etiquette for not being an asshole in general, anywhere. Westerners, especially white Westerners, have come to believe that if we're paying any amount of money for anything (whether it's an Egg McMuffin or a $8,000-a-night suite), then we're above the person providing it and can act however we want. But here's something particular about Hawai'i to keep in mind: white people colonized Hawai'i. Americans overthrew its monarchy in a coup. We stole their land and appropriated their culture and pushed their language into the margins. The Hawaiian economy is dependent upon tourism because we made it that way. And that waitress who you're throwing a Yelp hissy fit about (yes, a real example) because she was enjoying the local band playing instead of refilling your iced tea? She probably works two, maybe three jobs, because her rent and cost of living is so high, because tourism consumes an inordinate amount of the Islands' limited resources. Oh, and that Filipino valet taking "too long" to retrieve your car (refer to TripAdvisor for examples), or the Japanese gardener loudly trimming the bushes while you're trying to chill out on your lānai (again, see TripAdvisor, the Official Forum for Entitled Tourists)? There's an

excellent chance that person's family came to Hawai'i as indentured servants in the plantation era.

Listen, I get how uncomfortable the words "entitled" and "privileged" are for white people. It's difficult having them applied to us, either because our sense of privilege is woven so deep into our DNA that we don't recognize it, or because we *do* recognize it from time to time, sometimes think to question it, and then are totally embarrassed to admit to behaving in a way we think we condemn.

It would be completely disingenuous of me to pretend I've never acted like an entitled tourist myself, positive that because I paid a certain amount of money I deserved all the attention of a princess. I paid for paradise, goddamnit! Why isn't it quiet when I want it to be quiet, and why isn't my food here when I want it to be here? I often think back on a "how dare you ignore me when my tourist dollars (my dad's tourist dollars) are what keeps this place open" tantrum I threw when I was sixteen and the making of my ham sandwich was being ignored in favor of the Ed & Don's employee talking to a friend. My embarrassment over this rant was further exacerbated when, decades later, I found out Lauren's brother had worked at Ed & Don's during that era, and there was at least a possibility he was the one I was a total brat to. Oh, you mean there are human beings behind those counters? As I got older—and paid my own way (cough)—I came to realize that what I expect, what I think I'm entitled to, seemed directly proportionate to how much money I paid.

Tourists have imposed ourselves onto the Hawaiian culture, and our financial impact alone is not enough to make us beloved. (There's a difference between being necessary, and beloved, by the way, and I'm still puzzling over the areas of overlap that create the unique touristic definition of "appreciated." Tourists are often told they're *appreciated*.) While tourists' insolent behavior will undoubtedly beget negative consequences, you might not see them right away. The employees you've complained to might quickly refill your iced tea, or check on when your macnut-crusted mahi-mahi will come out, or even give you a discount on your bill with a toothy smile. This is what they need to do—are *told* to do—to survive. But make no mistake: they will talk story about boorish tourists to their friends, family, and coworkers until these tales infiltrate the groundwater. So the next time you get snubbed in an off-the-beaten-path market or a big pickup truck is riding on your bumper, it's because some tourist—whether it be you or someone else over the last one hundred years—was a dick.

5. The big pickup truck riding on your bumper is a confusing aspect of hōʻihi. This happens to me every single time I'm in Hawaiʻi, almost every single day. I'm doing the speed limit like a good tourist/responsible driver/old lady that I've become, and get tailgated by an impatient driver in a giant pickup or rusted Toyota with a kukui nut lei hanging from the rearview mirror. I tossed this conundrum out to Reverend Jim, who

was raised on Oʻahu. "I'm not supposed to speed, but I'm not going fast enough, either," I said. "What am I supposed to do?"

"Just pull over and let them pass you," he said. That had *never* occurred to me before, because on the mainland pulling over is equivalent to giving up in the blood sport of driving. In Hawaiʻi it's just showing respect—not assuming that whatever you're doing and the way you're doing it is the most important thing. There's a good chance that while you're tootling along to the beach or Starbucks or your sunset dinner reservation, that person behind you is trying to get to work, or just got off work, or—most likely—is tired of having to constantly make way for tourists. (On average, there are nearly twice as many visitors than residents on Maui, Kauaʻi, and the Big Island in a month.) That was Lauren's explanation when I asked why visitors can't win on the speed limit issue. "We're just looking for ways to be annoyed at tourists," she said.

And there's the rub: an epiphany that was at first incredibly uncomfortable, and then ultimately freeing for me. Unless I pack up my life and move to Hawaiʻi—and don't flee from island fever in less than a year—I will always be a tourist. I will always be an interloper. It doesn't matter how "cool" I act, or that I got a honu needled onto my skin, or that I recycle when I'm on island, or that I say "yeah?" and the end of every question, or that I have an extensive playlist of Hawaiian music on my iPod, or that I wrote a book about Hawai'i. I will always be a haole mainlander, and have to accept the assumptions made about me.

This is an unusual spot for white people to be in. We're used to being the ones making the rules, making the judgments, being in the majority and assuming it's our birthright to be treated with respect. Negative cultural judgments based on a superficial understanding of "who we are" is something people of color shoulder every day. And they didn't do anything other than be born brown, while white people have done plenty wrong. Oh, have we done *plenty* wrong. So I've accepted my derided status as a haole tourist—which is still a position of economic privilege, by the way. It's not like I'm being consigned to a shantytown.

It means that I can stop trying so fucking hard to blend in, to talk and walk like I "belong" in Hawai'i, to gain some sort of acceptance, because it's never gonna happen. I can—and try all the time to—be the best version of a tourist, one who gives hōʻihi, and encourages others to do the same. And what I've found is it's not that hard. It's not that bad. You're on vacation in Hawai'i, why are you in a hurry? Where you got to be so fast? Maybe there are times that the machinery of workers makes it noisier than you wish, but look over there—see those palm trees swaying, see that beckoning blue sky, see that majestic ocean? And maybe the seals or the turtles or the whales aren't where you want them to be, but can we just appreciate our divine fortune of sharing a planet with them at all?

Joan Didion said, "A place belongs forever to whoever claims it hardest, remembers it most obsessively, wrenches it from itself, shapes it, renders it, loves it so radically that he remakes it in his own image." There was a time that was appealing to me. That there was some way that I could love Hawaiʻi hard enough that it would be mine. But Hawaiʻi is not mine. It does not, nor should it ever belong to me. I consider myself honored to think there is even the smallest way in which I belong to it.

My husband contends that the people who most need a greater understanding—and therefore an attitude adjustment—about these realities won't seek it out. He suspects most tourists simply don't give a shit. But I'm not so sure. I think Yelling Guy might have been apologetic about his behavior if he understood it contextually. The woman who was peeved that the turtles weren't where she wanted them to be would be genuinely sad if she couldn't see them because they were extinct. And maybe those folks surrounding the honu would have been remorseful if they knew their actions were possibly contributing to the die-out of an endangered species. I also could be hopelessly, optimistically naïve. Either way, the next time *I* will know better. The next time I will walk into the shallow water and tell my fellow tourists that this graceful, ancient creature is not theirs. I will tell them to let it be free.

Da Kine | 'Aumakua

"WE CALL THOSE 'AUMAKUA,'" SAID THE WOMAN FROM Hawai'i who I met at a book fair in Seattle. She was referring to the honu tattooed on my upper arm. The tattoo was six months old, and she was the first—but not the last—person to refer to it that way.

'Aumakua are familial ancestral spirits that provide protection and strength. They often take the form of an animal—a shark, a gecko, an owl, a honu. Sometimes they appear in dreams, and sometimes in person, to give warnings, to give comfort, and to provide guidance and strength.

When asked the meaning of my tattoo, I sometimes tell people a long story that includes how honu always find their way home. When I published my first book, I wanted to call that meaning to me. I wanted to make sure that wherever the experience took me—whether readers loved or hated my book, whether I got glitzy attention or was virtually ignored—I'd still remember the friends who loved me no matter what. Home. The short story behind the meaning of my tattoo was that honu are a symbol of longevity, and since there wasn't a lot of that in my family (depending on who I was talking to, I might elaborate), I hoped for a long life. Sometimes I say that for years I'd been searching for some perfect piece of jewelry that would keep me connected to Hawai'i when I was back home. Pearls, shells, beads, earrings, necklaces, bracelets, plumeria, palm trees, honu. None of them ever carried the spirit, the mana, that I felt on island. They just made me feel like a tourist fulfilling the role of a consumer.

But is the honu truly my 'aumakua? They are said to belong to families. I no longer had a family. Maybe if we'd had an 'aumakua, my mom, dad, and brother would still be alive. I suppose I could weave the narrative that I am the only one to whom the 'aumakua revealed itself; that it came to me because I needed the most guidance, or because I held the most mana, or because I would be the one to survive, or some other inspiring origin story. And maybe that's the only difference between my honu being just a tattoo and being an 'aumakua. Whether or not I believe.

Return to the Kahala

THE FIRST TIME JOAN DIDION STAYED AT HONOLULU'S
Kahala Hilton in 1966, she found herself sitting on
the beach next to the Rolling Stones, who were "pale and
bored and facing away from the sea." She wrote about the
encounter for *Esquire* in 1976 after having just returned
from the Kahala, where Rod Stewart, Helen Reddy, Joe
Frazier, Olivia Newton-John, and George Kennedy were
also staying. Carol Burnett and the Queen of England
had just left (not together, one assumes), and Muhammad
Ali had just checked in. Frazier left the day Ali arrived, by
the way, so there was no Rumble in the Jungle on O'ahu.

The first time I stayed at the Kahala Hilton was 1979,
when I was twelve years old, and if anyone famous was
in the environs, my mom, dad, and brother didn't alert
me. I have very few memories of the Kahala, except for
watching dolphins swim in the lagoon in front of our
room's lānai. My first stay at the Kahala was also my first
excursion to Hawai'i, beginning a decades-long affair with
the Islands. I didn't know that at age twelve, just as I didn't
know six months later my mom and dad would divorce.
And what I really didn't know, couldn't know, wouldn't
have been able to go on living if I knew, was that by the
time I was twenty-six my mom would be dead, and by
forty-three my dad would be dead, and by forty-four my

brother would be dead, too. I didn't know that the next time I returned to the Kahala would be to scatter my dad's ashes along the shore.

* * *

Didion said that things tend to sort themselves out at the Kahala. It was a manageable place for her, and if you've spent any time reading Joan Didion you know that her psyche was often quite unmanageable. She was frequently a bundle of frayed nerves, obsessed with parents killing their children and children killing their parents, a recalcitrant adult, and rarely mindlessly happy. But at the Kahala she was mindlessly happy. She and her husband fled California to the Kahala to work, to write, to complete Hollywood scripts. She knew exactly what she was getting when she came down from her room after writing: an open-air lobby with teak parquet floors and fresh-cut orchids, longue chairs arranged on the beach and around the pool, guests who would watch her child and her pocketbook, and, most importantly, the sense that there was always someone who would take care of every need. "Nothing bad can reach me here," said Didion.

This is an entirely different mental state than when she stayed at the Royal Hawaiian on Waikīkī Beach, five miles away. At the Royal she was constantly aware of war and death, of the bodies at the bottom of Pearl Harbor and the bodies above Pearl Harbor in Punchbowl Cemetery. Perhaps the Kahala was just far enough away from all that for Didion to escape the haunting, to remain temporarily unaware.

When I returned to the Kahala (no longer a Hilton) thirty-seven years after my first visit, I was aware of too much. I was aware that a portion of my dad's ashes were in my carry-on bag and that I was detained at the Portland airport on suspicion that they contained "explosive agents." I explained my dad was a veteran. "I'm taking his ashes to Honolulu where he was stationed during WWII," I said. "Please just get this over with," I said, as a TSA agent felt under the folds of my breasts, between my legs, around my ass, as another TSA agent prepared to "test" my dad's ashes.

I was aware that a week earlier Donald Trump had been elected president. Protests and riots had seized US cities every day since. The night before I left for Honolulu, a white friend with three black children was walking home when someone leaned out a car window and screamed "nigger lover" and "dirty white woman," warning her, "We know where you live." A few hours later, someone broke into her house while she and her children hid in a locked bedroom. My friend called 911, but no police ever arrived. She reported this nerve-racking incident on Facebook, and the next morning her account was gone. I was rattled by the whole week's events—protests and hate crimes and fear and anger and grief—and I hoped that Hawai'i would restore some tensile strength to my psyche.

I was also aware that my husband and I kind of hate Honolulu. We retreat to Kaua'i once a year because it's relatively small and quiet and impossibly pretty. It doesn't have freeways, like the island of O'ahu, and therefore isn't choked by highway congestion. There are as many hotels on the 552 square miles of Kaua'i as on the one square mile of Waikīkī. But we went Honolulu so I could spread my dad's ashes and research this book I was writing. Some of the research would be about the history of colonialism in Hawai'i, and some would be about pop culture, and some would be about my own history of visiting Hawai'i. There was so much I didn't remember and no one alive to remind me. I hoped that revisiting the Kahala would rattle the deep storage of memory.

More than anything, I was aware that none of this sounded fun. None of it sounded like any of the reasons mainlanders usually come to Hawai'i: for relaxation and sun and adventure and pampering and an escape from the banalities of everyday life.

* * *

The ubiquitous Hilton chain is now the third-largest hotel group in the world, but in 1960 it didn't have a property anywhere in Hawai'i. When Conrad Hilton finally decided to build a luxury hotel in Honolulu, it seemed bizarre that the proposed site wasn't on popular Waikīkī Beach. Instead, the 12.5-acre parcel lay in a residential neighborhood called Wai'alae-Kāhala. With Waikīkī's cautionary tale of dreadful commercial sprawl just on the other side of Diamond Head, Wai'alae-Kāhala residents were vehemently opposed to Hilton's attempt to rezone their neighborhood for hotel use. They submitted over 1,200 written protests to the Honolulu Planning Commission, resulting in the Commission voting against the zoning change.

A lot of good that did, because the City Council ignored them and voted 7-0 to allow hotel zoning in Wai'alae-Kāhala. They cited the same justification used for every piece of tourist infrastructure in the state: it would be good for the economy. They were afraid that if they rejected the proposal, Hilton would pack up his toys and take them elsewhere.

Well, a lot of good *that* did, because the Honolulu mayor vetoed the bill to rezone the area. He had a "We don't bend over for Hilton" attitude about the whole proposition. He knew Hilton *had* to get into the Hawai'i market, because in the early 1960s it was the newest, hottest, most rapidly developing tourist destination in the country. If Hilton couldn't have the Wai'alae-Kāhala parcel, he'd find another place on O'ahu. The mayor believed the proposed hotel would not only compromise the quality of life for residents, he also postulated that any guest willing to pay a luxury price for a hotel wouldn't want to be trapped in a residential neighborhood near the hustle and bustle of the city. They would want isolation.

Well, you guessed it—a lot of good that did, too. The City Council overrode the mayor's veto, and Hilton commenced with the construction of the Kahala Hilton. It cost $12 million to build, equivalent to about $86 million now. The guest rooms were the largest in Hawai'i, at over five hundred square feet, boasting gigantic bathrooms with separate his and hers dressing areas and vanities. A placid saltwater lagoon was installed between the swimming pool and the buildings, one hundred and fifty thousand cubic yards of white sand were barged over from Moloka'i to create the pristine beach, and two lava rock peninsulas were built at each end to protect the shore. When all was said and done, the cost per room was $33,000—at least $18,000 more than most other island hotels.

When the hotel opened in 1964, rooms started at $32.50 per night. This seems quaint now, but back then it was a price too steep for most travelers. The hotel's infancy was plagued by 20 percent occupancy. Then, in 1966, NBC hosted its annual meeting at the Kahala, filling the entire hotel with TV stars. Word of the luxurious accommodations spread quickly among the celebrity set, and by 1967 the hotel was regularly at 90 percent occupancy. In 1976, Didion said it was often booked a year in advance.

It turned out the odd location was exactly what guests craved. They were secluded, but not isolated. This quality is the magic exponent of Hawai'i itself. A six-hour flight is all that separates Honolulu from the West Coast, meaning you don't have to leave before the sun comes up and you arrive before the sun goes down. "One dials out of here direct," Didion wrote—today's equivalent of having a strong cellphone signal and Wi-Fi. Staying connected to the business and news of the mainland is part of the draw. The other part of the draw is that after you hear the news or negotiate the business deal, you hang up the phone or close your computer and find yourself suspended in what Didion referred to as a "temporal paradise," where the sky is always blue, or soon to be blue, if you happen to get caught under passing clouds releasing the rain that keeps Hawai'i green. Palm trees perpetually sway in the trade winds, with white plumeria and firecracker red ginger setting the scene. The temperature rarely falls below sixty-five degrees or soars above ninety, most often hovering at some Eden-like in between. If you do get too hot? Then just wade into the Pacific, which is always turquoise or azure or cerulean or some other artists' name. And, when you are staying at the Kahala, someone will take care of your needs—a whole team of people will attend to your needs—regardless of whether it's 1966 or 1979 or 2016.

* * *

Memory is a fickle beast. Even though I couldn't summon many visions, ideas, feelings about my first stay at the Kahala in 1979, I was sure they'd come rushing back when my husband and I returned in 2016. Those memories would fill these pages, and they would fill some of the gaps created when my mom and dad and brother died.

Is this familiar? I asked myself as Michael drove down a narrow street toward the hotel. Mid-century modern condos on one side, a golf course on the other, palm trees all around, the ocean over there. Do these sights, these smells, this ether remind me of the only other time I was here? Nothing was jarred loose—not on Kahala Road, not as we passed the discreet signage for the hotel, not as we pulled into the porte-cochère, and not as we entered the ornate lobby.

The Kahala is described as "unabashedly modern," "old world," "relaxed," and "a fantasyland" by guide books and magazines. It is, somehow, all those things. It's a mixed-media painting, where materials are layered and peeled back and raised and revealed. The base structure of the hotel consists of ten rectangular stories of white concrete. This bare, Brutalist form is where the design of many hotels over in Waikīkī ends. But at the Kahala, a trellis creates a second stratum, climbing up the building in a modern lattice of right angles and rectangles, meeting in a pergola over the roof. The trellis looks like white steel, but is actually made of reinforced concrete. All this would look unbearably cold and flat if it weren't for the white semicircle balconies protruding outward. The dreamy mezzalunas break up all those hard lines, all those right angles, giving the impression that each room extends out into the lush mountains or the cerulean sea.

The Kahala lobby is often described as "pavilion-like" because of its thirty-foot-high ceilings. You'd be hard-pressed to find an upscale hotel in Hawai'i—or anywhere, really—that doesn't boast thirty-foot-high ceilings. High ceilings are what let you know you're in a *grand* hotel. That, and ornate chandeliers. The design of the Kahala's chandeliers most exemplify the hotel's melding of the old and the new. Giant and pear-shaped, they each sport around fifty curving branches of oxidized bronze ending in candelabra bulbs. The base of the fixtures is fairly Victorian, except that each bulb is covered by a clear glass globe, ushering the aesthetic into the early twentieth century. Dangling from each chandelier are twenty-eight thousand rectangles of colored glass. The cobalt, emerald, topaz, amethyst, turquoise, and moonstone fused glass transforms the otherwise sedate lobby into a prismatic slice of sixties psychedelia.

But none of it was familiar to me. I took pictures of the chandeliers and the high archways and the shabby-chic rattan couches as we waited for our luggage. Michael and I are self-sufficient travelers and usually park our own car and carry our own bags, but I wanted to experience the Kahala the way my dad might have when he treated his family. We were standing at the elevator listening to the bellman tell us where the spa and the gift shop and the restaurants and other places to spend money are, and that's when it happened: I looked down the hall towards the gift shop, and I knew I had been there. I don't know why I was in this hallway in 1979 (apparently, the gift shop was located elsewhere back then), but it was familiar on a cellular level. It reminds me of that YouTube video of an elephant looking into a mirror for the first time and recognizing that the image reflected back is him. It gave me hope that, over the next few days, my past would return to me.

* * *

After the bellman gave us a *thorough* tour of our room ("This is the switch for the fan," "This is your flat-screen TV," "These are your two sinks"), we went downstairs to grab a late lunch from the bar by the pool. It wasn't entirely obvious how to get to the pool, but we did what seemed logical: got off the elevator at the lobby. It turns out the back of the lobby is raised thirty-eight feet above ground, so we wandered down a curved staircase towards the lower foyer. A middle-aged black man sat on a couch at the bottom of the stairs. Protests and riots and hate crimes and my friend being harassed and robbed flashed through me. I wanted to make sure to look this man in the eyes and smile, a gesture that in the past would have made me feel like a pandering white liberal, but the election had changed the rules. Everything felt so precarious, with the line between tolerance and hate so thin. It was important to declare which side of it I was on. I smiled at him and he smiled back, and then I spotted the door outside and headed for it. Michael was following me, because he still expected me to have more of an idea where we were going. I passed the grand atrium for the ballrooms and heard a guy say something like, "Oh, is she here?"

I pushed through the door to the sunshine. All the reasons tourists come to Hawai'i were in front of me: a waterfall gushing over black lava rock, a lagoon inhabited by dolphins and sea turtles, coconut palm trees, cabanas shading lounge chairs, the blue ocean, and fluffy white clouds.

Michael jogged to my side. "You know we just walked by Ben Stiller, right?" he said.

"Get out!" I looked behind me to where I heard the guy speak, but only saw the reflection of palm trees and clouds in the glass door. I'd had very few celebrity encounters in my life, and none with the star power of Ben Stiller. The closest I'd come was riding an elevator with Michael Landon at the Royal Hawaiian Hotel when I was thirteen.

Michael and I sat at a wicker table in wicker chairs on a floor made of sand and ordered fish tacos and mai tais, because we are never truly in Hawai'i until we're drinking mai tais. Ben Stiller sat down one table over from ours with two people we didn't recognize. I watched how the waiter acted with him, which was exactly how he acted with us: hello, would you like something to drink, is there anything else I can get for you, have a nice day. My eyes followed him back to the server station. As far as I could tell, he didn't discuss his famous customer with the other waiters. No one huddled or whispered or even snuck sly glances. They just went about their jobs.

When I checked the internet to see why Ben Stiller was on island, I discovered a social media site devoted to revealing filming locations in Hawai'i:

> *Just a reminder there's a movie coming to town reportedly this week called "Brad's Status". It stars Ben Stiller & Luke Wilson and it's being produced by Brad Pitt. If you see or hear anything even a rumor inbox us.*

I didn't "inbox" them. Didion said the public relations director for the Kahala saw it as her job to make "sure the guests have what they want and the *National Enquirer* does not." Leaving each other comfortably alone feels inherent in the social contract of staying at the Kahala.

* * *

I quickly forgot all my original reasons for being there, on the island. Research for my book and spreading my dad's ashes took a backseat to escaping the post-election chaos, to wanting to be temporarily unaware. Michael and I spent the first day by the pool. I swam and dozed in the sun and watched honu swim in the lagoon. The honu were born in captivity, but would be released into the ocean at age two, innately equipped with the skills to survive. I turned the green honu tattooed on my upper arm toward the honu in the lagoon, as if they could commune.

After lunch I needed to use the bathroom. The pool attendant directed me to a path between the bar and the lagoon. I experienced my second flash: *I have been here before.* With my mom, in our bathing suits, her leading me, me following. This is not much—just a mom and daughter going to the ladies' room together—but it's a memory of my mom I'd never had before. It returned a piece of her to me.

* * *

It didn't occur to us that we'd need reservations for dinner in our own hotel on a Thursday night, but such is Honolulu. At the Italian restaurant, we were told there wasn't a free table but were welcome to sit at the bar. It was only four stools along a recessed counter, trapping the bartender in a cube outfitted with a blender and ice. Our bartender's nametag read "James," but everyone called him Jimmy. He was young—about twenty-five—and had graduated from the University of Hawaiʻi with a degree in graphic design. He knew an astounding amount about food and wine—like, he could tell you stories about specific grapes varietals in Alba, Italy, or the history of Parmigiano-Reggiano cheese.

I asked Jimmy if the staff got special training on how to handle celebrities.

"Not really," he shrugged as he wiped out a glass. "You just treat them like everyone else. That's why they come here." You don't take pictures, ask for autographs, or blather on about how much you loved them in whatever film.

Jimmy was only star struck once: when Pierce Brosnan dined at the restaurant. It wasn't even his presence that made Jimmy flutter; it's that when Brosnan's drink order came to him, it was for a dry martini. "I was making a martini for James Bond," he said, laughing. "That really got me."

I refrained from asking whether it was shaken or stirred.

* * *

The next day I tried to get back on track with research. It gave me a sense of purpose in a place where I, a tourist, had rarely had purpose before. For almost forty years, my only role in Hawai'i had been to wade in the ocean and lie by the pool and make out with blond boys on beaches. I spent money on hotel rooms and mai tais and shave ice, on T-shirts and trinkets to take back home. But research gave me a mission. Never mind that the research happened to be visiting the same sights *The Brady Bunch* had in 1972—a purpose not exactly laden with gravitas. I came to the Islands with questions to be answered, with stories to be written, with *The End* and *Goodbye* waiting to be whispered.

I stood in front of the eighteen-foot bronze statue of King Kamehameha I, which appeared less imposing in real life than in pictures. In pictures you rarely see that it stands in front of the four-story clock tower of the Hawai'i' Supreme Court, which somewhat dwarfs its majesty. Kitty-corner from the statue, I toured the

Renaissance-style ʻIolani Palace. I took in the Grand Hall and the Throne Room, the Blue Room and the Music Room, and the bedroom where Queen Liliʻuokalani was imprisoned after the colonialist coup. This room displayed the 97-by-94-inch quilt she painstakingly sewed, her panels documenting the loss of Hawaiʻi. Next door to all this rich history and classical design is the modern State Capitol building. The Capitol edifice is all straight lines, all concrete. It is surrounded by a reflecting pool meant to evoke the Pacific Ocean. Its cone-shaped legislative chambers symbolize volcanoes. The building's columns are supposed to represent palm trees—but really just look like columns—and inside, two chandeliers represent the moon and the sun. Everything at the Capitol is a stand-in for Hawaiʻi's true beauty.

After touring the Capitol Mall, we made the intrepid adventure to Waikīkī. I wanted to visit the Sheraton—not usually a sightseeing destination, like the Royal Hawaiian next door. Built in 1971, the Sheraton Waikiki is thirty-eight stories of boxy concrete. It's also the hotel the Brady family stayed at, and the only Waikīkī hotel where my family ever stayed. I slept there during spring break in 1980, and not again, because I'm not a fan of Waikīkī. But it's where my brother went after he graduated from high school and met the woman who would be his girlfriend for five years. The Sheraton was our home base whenever my dad and brother and I made day trips to Honolulu from Maui. In 1984, we flew over to see Notre Dame play SMU in the Aloha Bowl, and ate the Sheraton breakfast buffet before continuing to the stadium. In 1987, my dad had

meetings in Honolulu, so I flew over with him and spent
the day at the Sheraton. I laid on the beach and listened
to my Walkman, ate lunch, and window-shopped while
my dad negotiated real-estate transactions. After lunch I
sat on a banquette in the lobby and wrote in my journal:
There's a lot of things you can think about in a place like this, I
wrote. *I'm always thinking about where I'm going next. I'm
always planning my escape.*

Waikīkī is such a paradox. When you're on the streets,
you could be in Phoenix or Dallas or Miami. High-rise
office buildings converge on you. There's a Cheesecake
Factory and a Sunglass Hut, a Forever 21 and a KFC.
There are crowds—lordy, are there crowds. Walking, driving, sitting, standing. This is why I find Waikīkī entirely
pointless. It's just a city, and there's no reason anyone
should fly thousands of miles to experience it. But on the
other side of this metropolitan madness is a different kind
of madness, one that is distinctly Hawai'i: the actual beach
itself. Yes, it's lined with too many hotels and is crowded
with too many people, but it is the Hawai'i of postcards. A
white sand beach stretches for two miles, with the effusive
Diamond Head crater bursting at the end. Gentle waves
beckon to outrigger canoes and surfboards waiting to be
set into action. Children build sandcastles from buckets
and shovels bought in hotel lobbies, and the smell of coconut sunscreen permeates it all.

Michael took my picture in the Sheraton's porte-cochère, because my dad took a picture of me in the same
spot in 1987. Comparing them, I saw that I am heavier
now, paler, and less new-wave than in 1987. The differences

between the pictures weren't just due to the aesthetics of aging, though. The pictures confirmed that the years I spent in Hawai'i with my dad and brother during the eighties were a separate life. I was young and free, and even without my mom there, we were a family. I became a different person after they died, alone, but not alone. Aware of all this mortality.

The lobby of the Sheraton is a rotunda, with the check-in desk curving along the outer arc. When Michael and I walked from the bright outdoors to the dim inside, I saw my dad as clear as day. He was standing in line with our luggage, wearing white pants and an aloha shirt patterned with red plumeria. I spotted the banquettes where I wrote in my journal. We came across the lānai where my family ate the breakfast buffet. Touring the Sheraton didn't wallop me with melancholy or bewilderment, like at the Kahala. It was more like discovering something I always suspected was true: my soul connection to Hawai'i started there, not at the Kahala. The Kahala was the end of my parents' marriage. The end of my childhood. The Sheraton launched and cradled a different love. One that was more abiding, more encompassing. These islands.

* * *

I didn't bring all my dad's ashes with me to Honolulu. I'd intended to, and two nights before we left Portland tried to transfer them out of their metal urn into a plastic bag. The Asian urn wasn't poised somewhere dignified in my house, like on the mantle or an elegant side table. It was in a cardboard box, in a storage cabinet, in my garage. When

I cleaned out my dad and Steve's house in Denver, I didn't know what to do with their ashes. They were too heavy, too cumbersome physically and emotionally to carry back to Portland. So I wrapped them in bubble wrap and put them in a box that a friend shipped to me. When they arrived, I was too bereft to contemplate them or their proper place. I put them in the garage, and that's where they'd rested for six years. I never even removed the bubble wrap.

When I retrieved my dad's ashes before our flight to Honolulu, they were heavier than when I'd picked them up from the mortuary. Back then, they seemed so light, so *slight* for the entire life of a man. I wondered where I should complete this task, the transfer from urn to bag. If some ashes were to spill, would it be better to spill on the floor, or a table, or a counter? If I had to clean ashes from the floor, they would inevitably get mixed with dust and cat hair. A clean kitchen counter left more chance of keeping them pure.

It was harder than I expected. The neck of the urn was narrow, the mouth of the Ziploc bag wide, but floppy. I tried to hold the heavy urn up and the bag open, but I really needed two more hands. I purposefully did this when Michael wasn't home, because it's a lot to ask of anyone, even my husband of twenty-two years. My dad's ashes *did* spill. Not a lot—perhaps a few tablespoons, if that's how you measure human remains. They fell onto the counter and into the sink, and I realized I was going to have to wash my dad's ashes down the drain because there was no way to retrieve them from the sink. The gallon Ziploc was already bursting with weight, and there was still plenty left in the urn and my hands were shaking and my brain was shaking like weak LSD kicking in. And I realized: I can't do this.

I called my friend Jen, whose mom died six months after my dad. She talked me through rinsing the ashes down the drain. She explained that *of course* I was freaking out, I hadn't even touched the urn in over six years, and suddenly I'm moving ashes from one container to the next so I can put them in my carryon luggage like they're Cheez-Its.

"You don't have to take them with you," Jen said. "Deal with them some other time, when it feels right."

"We're paying thousands of dollars to fly there and stay at this expensive hotel just so I can scatter these damn ashes!" I said. "What the hell kind of idea was that?"

"You're also going to do research," she reminded me.

"I don't even know what research looks like anymore," I said. "What am I going to do, visit every place the Brady Bunch visited when they were in Honolulu?"

"Sure, why not?" she said. "Besides, it'll be good to get away from the political horror show here."

As Jen told me about the status of her mom's remains— she constantly moved them from room to room—I examined my dad's ashes on the counter. How would I get them off, into the bag? They would stick to a rag, a sponge, a paper towel. I retrieved a credit card from my wallet and used the edge to sweep all the ashes into a pile. And then, without forethought, and even though it had been thirty years since I'd done cocaine, I divvied them up into thin, neat rails.

"Oh my god, you'll never believe what I just did," I told Jen.

"Please don't snort them!" she pleaded.

"That's too morbid, even for me." I set down my credit card. "I've got to clean this up before Michael gets home." I could picture it—*I hope you had a good day, honey! And by the way, here's my dead dad all over our kitchen.*

Jen suggested I take only some of the ashes with me, but if spreading them didn't feel okay, it was fine to bring them back home. That made the most sense. I scooped enough to fit in a quart-sized Ziploc and sealed that within another Ziploc, and put the rest back in the garage. And that is what got me frisked by airport security.

* * *

On our last night in Honolulu, Michael and I took my dad's ashes in their bag-within-a-bag to the Kahala beach at sunset. Magenta orchid leis hung limply from my arm. I slipped off my sandals and waded into the water up to my ankles, and I opened the Ziploc bag and I turned it upside down. The ashes turned the water cloudy. It never looked that way in movies. When cinematic mourners dump remains into the sea, the ashes appear as heavenly particles, like dust motes captured in rays of light. This dirty gray was more like runny concrete. I gently placed the orchid leis over the murky cloud, and walked back to Michael. In my head I sang a verse from Leonard Cohen's "Hallelujah," the one about doing my best, and telling the truth, and everything still going wrong. So fucking wrong. But, somehow, I managed to march forward. The solution, the secret, the magic for soldiering on lies in the unreliable partnership that creates memory. It's in the exponent we call faith.

Michael and I stood, arms around each other, and I shed a few tears as the leis drifted away, they drifted with the currents, they drifted right into the lava rocks of the man-made peninsula a few yards away. The leis were stuck in the eddies between rocks. "I don't know what to do about that," I said.

We walked out onto the peninsula, and Michael scrambled down the lava to retrieve the soggy leis. "Okay," I said. "Let's try this again." The flowers were light and airy, so I knew I'd have to throw them hard. I wound up my right arm like a softball pitch and heaved the leis into the sea. This time they caught a current that carried them out, away, towards Diamond Head. The sun set behind the sparkling cone, bathing the world in lambent light.

"Excuse me," a young guy behind us said. "Will you take our picture?" He pointed to his girlfriend, maybe his fiancée, his new wife. He had no idea what we'd just done, what we were watching. He probably thought we were just admiring the sunset like everyone else. It was too awkward, too awful, to tell him. Nothing bad should reach this young couple here. Michael took their picture while I tried to keep an eye on the leis, as they got smaller and more remote. He re-joined me at my side.

"You kind of want to tell them, 'This is what for better or for worse looks like, kids,'" I said. Soon, we could no longer see the leis. The sky was indigo and the clouds were pink, and tiki torches lit our way back inside.

* * *

Things tend to sort themselves out at the Kahala, Didion said, but I don't know what got sorted out for me. Ashes and family and Hawaiian history and political angst and memory all jockeyed for position in my emotional Jenga, but nothing found a resting place. But what did I expect? To feel completely at peace with my family's demise, with being the keeper of their memories but incapable of remembering it all? With part of my dad—and all of my brother—still sitting in a box in my garage because I can't stand to have them inside, but can't stand to let them go, either? That when I returned to the mainland, the political chaos would have sorted itself out, or, at least, that I could engage with it calmly? No, the best I could hope for was that the elements of my frayed psyche might become more manageable.

When we returned to Portland, Jen asked if we'd visit Honolulu again. I said it wasn't likely. The city was too crowded and loud, and nothing drew us there, not like Kaua'i. But as months passed, I dreamed of the Kahala with increasing frequency. I floated through the prism of chandeliers, and swayed with insouciance in the trade winds and palm trees. I waded into the lambent horizon towards memories of my mom. I swam in the lagoon with honu, graceful sun-seekers who always find their way home.

Da Kine | Mana

QUEEN LILIʻUOKALANI HAD MANA. THE ʻĀINA HAS mana. Senator Daniel K. Inouye had it, hula has it, and legendary North Shore surfer Eddie Aikau *definitely* had it. Mana is power, but not in the "I have lots of money" way, or the "I can control you" way, or the "I own your means of production and living" way that motivated the white colonialists. Mana is spiritual power, energetic power, power that can't be seen but can be felt.

Mana is in the land. Mana is in words. Mana is in dance. It is in whatever connects our spirit to the worldly elements. Mana is what makes people strong in the face of fear, what makes them compassionate—to their own people and to others—what connects them to the earth and the water and the sky. It is strength and it is grace. Mana carries the stories of all the ancestors before us. It carries the story of the land. It is not limited to the chosen, the special, the holy. In ancient times it was believed that the highest aliʻi possessed the most mana, but the modern belief is that anyone can obtain it, be open to it, receive it, if they do right (called "pono"). To tell it in *Star Wars*: mana is the Force.

I felt the mana at Kāneiolouma, an ancient village in Poʻipū being unearthed and restored behind Brennecke's Beach Broiler restaurant and bar. As I stood in front of a tall kiʻi (which looks like a tiki/totem pole), something told me to sit down and close my eyes. I sat cross-legged on the flat, red stone engraved with petroglyphs of a canoe,

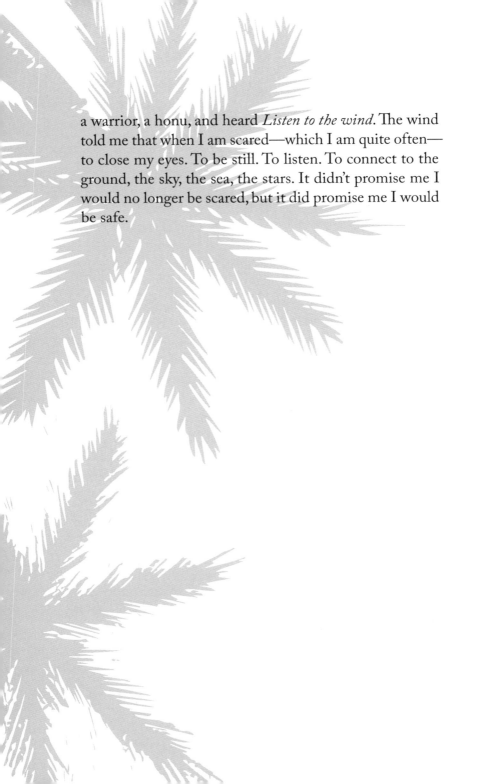

a warrior, a honu, and heard *Listen to the wind*. The wind told me that when I am scared—which I am quite often—to close my eyes. To be still. To listen. To connect to the ground, the sky, the sea, the stars. It didn't promise me I would no longer be scared, but it did promise me I would be safe.

Return to Maui

L AUREN AND I ATE FISH TACOS AT A SIDEWALK TABLE masquerading as an upside-down surfboard, with a yellow tail fin curving into the air. This stubby board probably couldn't float for one minute in the turquoise waves of Maui, but it made me feel like we were hanging out in a chill surfing town. It's been a pretty long time since Kīhei was a chill surfing town. The population has more than tripled since my dad and brother and I first visited in 1981, and it's now overrun with condos and tourists. In case I needed tangible proof of how this explosion had transformed the vibe, a thin woman walking by Lauren and me shouted, "This is the 808, man, and the government [pointing to the sky] is keeping track of you, they've got their alien devices up there and they know what you're doing so you better watch out, and I am *not* crazy!"

Lauren watched after her with soft eyes. "She gets kicked out of the coffee house all the time. Totally cracked out. It's really sad."

Not everyone would be as compassionate as Lauren. "Crazy bitch" and "fuckin' crack addict" no doubt lingered on other bystander's tongues. But Lauren had watched her own older brother go from being a promising doctor, to an opioid addict, to a meth addict, to the casualty of a self-inflicted gunshot to the head.

* * *

Lauren and I had only met for the first time in real life
a week earlier, but we had known each other via email
and social media and texts for nine years. We first came
into each other's lives in 2008, when the agency where
Lauren worked represented my novel. It was about a twenty-something guy confronting his repressed attraction to
other men while reeling from his bipolar brother's suicide.
I'm not sure why that—sexuality, identity, suicide—was
the prism I chose for telling the story of grief. My mom
died from emphysema when I was twenty-six, but that's
not the same as losing a sibling to mental illness. I know
that now.

After her brother committed suicide, Lauren left the
agency and moved back to Maui, where she grew up. She
dodged in and out of social media, and so went our communication. But there was something about knowing we
both loved Hawai'i, and we'd both lost our brothers, that
kept us connected across the Pacific, beyond the ether.

That week—the first time we'd met in real life—was
my first return to Maui in twenty-three years. I'd always
assumed I'd scatter my dad and brother's remains off
Wailea Beach, where we'd stayed a dozen times when I
was a teen. But anxiety sidelined me every time I tried
to plan an ash-scattering trip. I feared my family's ghosts
would lurk around every corner, threatening to strangle
me with grief. I'd made and cancelled reservations twice in
the previous few years; other attempts never even got that
far. Just looking at hotel and flight possibilities felt beyond
my abilities, as if I was trying to configure a polarimeter

for the telescope atop Haleakalā. I was only able to pull off this journey because my friend Michelle met me on Maui for the majority of the week, and we counted it as a "celebrating the year we turn fifty vacation." I counted it as "I know she won't let me fall off the face of the earth." Michelle had flown back home the night before Lauren and I had our second meeting, at Coconut's Fish Cafe.

Lauren is haole, with super blonde hair and freckles and icy blue eyes. What surprised me most about meeting her in person was that those blue eyes are warm and innocent, and also wise. She's twelve years younger than I am, and the first time I was on Maui in 1979 is the same year she was born in San Luis Obispo. Six years later, while I was drinking virgin daiquiris at the InterContinental Hotel, Lauren's dad came to Maui for a construction job and decided to move his family there. I like to pretend there was some way our families intersected back then, that perhaps her dad worked construction on the subdivision my dad was building, or maybe I spied blonde little Lauren building sandcastles on the beach. But the reality is that we were no one to each other back then.

Lauren's family settled onto five rugged acres at Oneuli Beach, adjacent to Makena on South Maui. Back in those days, this was out in the middle of nowhere. Their house was a former WWII lookout shelter: five hundred square feet with one cut-out window in the wall and a toilet in the middle of the room. They didn't have running water or electricity for their first few months, and the rotted-out floors were repaired with extra tin from the nearby pineapple canning plant. "My mom started bawling when we first arrived," Lauren said.

Who could blame her? It's certainly not the digs non-Unabomber folks dream of when moving to Hawai'i. Where's the wrap-around lānai and plantation-style windows inviting in the trade winds? Where are the banana and papaya trees that you just step outside to pick? Where is the greenery, the lushness, the Eden? Lauren's mom created their paradise. She painted the walls of the lookout shelter with palm trees and vines and waves, and adorned the pink bathroom door with a blonde mermaid who I image was, is, will always be, Lauren.

Painted on the wall at Coconut's Fish Cafe's is a palm tree shading a fish sandwich—a whole, grimacing fish between the top and bottom bun—with a cat holding a fishing pole above it. Coconut's is one of those restaurants that's sort of fast food, and sort of not. You stand in line to order, but the food is brought to your table. It's not particularly fast, but you eat with plastic utensils and paper napkins. Back in the eighties, my brother Steve and I had to drive thirty minutes to Kahului if we wanted fast food. Mostly we ate at hotel restaurants or one of the steak & seafood houses in Kīhei. There wasn't a single chain restaurant back then. Now Kīhei hosts the whole range of mainland staples: McDonald's, Taco Bell, Round Table, Jack in the Box, and a Subway. If you want to be waited on, there's Denny's, Ruby Tuesday, an Outback Steakhouse, and a Ruth's Chris (begging the question of how many steakhouses a town of twenty-three thousand needs). Even though I was aware that the town had changed over the past two decades, I told Lauren it was the proliferation of chain restaurants that surprised me the most.

"I remember how excited I was when the McDonald's opened," she said.

"So is it considered progress?" I asked.

She shrugged. "More locals go to someplace like Ruby Tuesday than tourists do," she said. "Not many people who live here can afford to eat at Kō."

A week earlier, we'd dined at Kō in the Fairmont Hotel. There's something particularly telling about how much an establishment will charge for appetizers, an entirely optional quick bite to tide you over with drinks. The cheapest appetizer at Kō was $19 (for lumpia, calamari, or BBQ pork skewers), and the most expensive was $26 (Kobe beef poke or seared ahi). At Ruby Tuesday, everything is literally half as expensive than it is at Kō. Kō is also set at a dreamy open-air resort, while Ruby Tuesday is in a strip mall with a Safeway and a bank. At Kō, the farm-to-fork flavors are perfectly balanced by its internationally acclaimed chef, with service striking that delicate balance between laid-back without being inattentive, and friendly without seeming like your waiter's having a manic episode. It's a special-occasion place, and meeting Lauren for the first time was a special occasion.

* * *

Lauren's family moved to Maui in 1985, which I consider to be the year right before the geography of the island radically changed. There were still no condos or hotels or shops or restaurants south of the InterContinental Hotel, my family's home base. Makena Beach was virtually deserted, and a four-wheel-drive truck was the safest means of navigating the deeply rutted road to access it. My brother risked taking our rental sedan when we'd go with our local friend, Bobby, and we were pretty lucky not to cause any damage to the undercarriage. I don't think we ever went there without Bobby; even with our "we're practically locals" delusion, we knew Makena didn't belong to us.

It turns out Makena could belong to anyone—for a price. You'd think that, as the daughter of a developer, it wouldn't have surprised me that an outsider would dare to erect a hotel just north of pristine Makena Beach. A Japanese investor opened the Maui Prince in 1986 as it expanded its resort portfolio throughout Hawai'i. By 1992, Japanese corporations owned 61 percent of all upscale hotel rooms in the state. You don't have to be all that clever to draw parallels between the Japanese real estate raid of the 1980s and the military attack of 1941, or to spot the metaphor of Lauren living in a former lookout for Japanese invasion at the very time they were gobbling up land on South Maui.

I sometimes draw a mental picture of the four miles of coastline between where I stayed in Wailea and Lauren's house at Oneuli Beach. My cartography is etched in December of 1991, and on one end my brother and I are checking out Tsunami, the nightclub of the new $650 million Grand Hyatt next door to the InterContinental. The resort's ornate design scheme is a combination of Hawaiian chic meets a rococo hangover, with marble statues spouting water, forty-foot ceilings painted with frescos, a fake volcano, and a gigantoid swimming complex with nine pools on six levels. Steve and I sit at Tsunami's marble bar—rumored to cost $1 million—and drink cocktails while a laser light show shoots around a conspicuously empty dance floor. "Tsunami!" we say in high-pitched voices, and then "Tsunami," in deep menacing voices, and then "Tsunami," in drunken who-knows-what-we-were-going-for voices. The word seems so silly to us, because the whole hotel seems silly. We are out of place in the overly gilded environment, and we've never felt out of place on Maui before.

Four miles down the coast from me and Steve is ten-year-old Lauren playing on five acres amid egrets, mongooses, kiawe, angel trumpets, feral cats, ancient Hawaiian temples, gravestones and ghosts. She is all white-blonde hair and lanky limbs. A Native Hawaiian named Charlie Kalani owns the land and, despite Japanese investors creeping in from all sides, he only charges Lauren's family an unfathomable $1,500 a *year* to live there. Lauren's dad has built a small detached cottage—called an 'ohana—for her brothers, accessed from the main house by a plywood "bridge" (the dubious quotes belong to Lauren). The family owns a TV, but it doesn't always get reception. They pool their leftover change in a jar, and when there's enough they rent a VCR from a shop in Kīhei and eat fried Cheerios and brown sugar sandwiches while watching movies.

Steve and I sit at one end of the progress, Lauren and her brothers at the other. We don't know of each other's existence in even the slightest way. What we really can't know is that when we finally meet for dinner twenty-five years later, halfway between Tsunami and Oneuli Beach, Lauren's brother Scott and my brother Steve will be dead. And we'll both just be getting to a point where we can live with that.

* * *

Steve never held a real job, as he crashed through decades of undiagnosed mental illness that he relentlessly tried to quell with alcohol. He sometimes worked for my dad, he played golf with his buddies, and he gained the weight that happens when former athletes stop chasing balls down fields and courts and spends more time at a bar than a gym. Steve got married and divorced and never had kids, both a tragedy and a blessing. A blessing because no innocent, malleable souls had to suffer their dad drinking and dying young; a tragedy because, in his finest moments, Steve was a gentle giant. At the InterContinental, kids in the Luau Pool would climb onto Steve's 6'4" frame and push him under water. He'd hold his breath and make them wait…five, six, seven…and then rise fast, like a sea monster, throwing the kids all directions into the pool. They'd scream and laugh and swim back to him to do it again and again.

Lauren's brother was a doctor, which sounds entirely different from Steve. Scott went to the universities and earned the degrees and completed the residency and worked in an ER where he saved and lost lives, but, like Steve, he didn't know how to keep one job, one love. Scott was driving from Kentucky to Colorado, between girl-friends, between jobs, when his truck broke down. He was standing over the engine when it exploded. Even before the explosion scorched 27 percent of Scott's body, he'd struggled with tequila and drugs. After the scorching, his brain, his nerves, his body had no chance.

Steve's decades of alcoholism and athleticism led to the total degeneration of his hip bones, but his mental illness kept him from having his hips replaced, or anything else that might fix his broken body, much less his broken mind. He could not get out of bed. He couldn't even sit up. His legs swelled to twice their normal size, and his skin blistered with infectious ulcers. Steve became addicted to prescription opioids. So did Scott.

They were tormented not just by their bodies, but also their minds. They took more drugs, different drugs—anything to mediate their fucked-up reality. Steve tried to knock himself out nearly every minute of the day, while Scott tried to rev himself back into life. They both had moments of recovery, grace, normalcy, almost-health. Steve had his hips replaced, and briefly walked again. Scott went to Maui and whispered to the ocean. Lauren and I stood on their feet while they danced, little girls gazing up towards our big brothers.

Then Steve went back to bed and benzos, and Scott returned to the mainland and meth. Their bodies buckled and their minds cracked until they were nothing but their own open wounds.

Steve didn't succumb to an overdose, as I assumed he would, or any of the vicious infections that ravaged his body, threatening to choke his essential organs. He had just gotten out of the hospital from one of these overdoses, some of these infections, and was sleeping, or not sleeping—who knows for sure what he did at 3:00 a.m.?—when two blood clots broke loose from his femoral vein and raced to his lungs. My brother was alone when he died.

Scottie was surrounded when he died—by his girlfriend and their drugs and by police rifles trained on the tangled web of paranoia in his brain. His girlfriend said that Scott's body was loaded with bourbon and methadone and Valium and sleeping pills and Lidocaine, and they were arguing about money and work and guilt and pain. His girlfriend said Scott threatened to shoot his beloved dogs—maybe threatened to shoot her—so she called 911. She said the SWAT team came. She said he put a gun in his mouth and pulled the trigger.

These are the stories Lauren and I were told. Our brothers both died in Colorado—a straight ten miles from each other—but we were thousands of miles away. We had to rely on other people to tell us what happened, to fill in our gaps. When Lauren pressed The Girlfriend for more details, she became defensive and said, "All you really need to know is that he is no longer trapped in a body that caused him ceaseless pain." As if that knowledge could be enough to alleviate our pain, our questioning. But the fractured way our brothers lived the last years of their lives meant the truth would be forever fractured, too. Lauren and I would never know, really, how and why they died.

After Steve died—one year after my dad died, and seventeen years after my mom died—I plunged into a depressive abyss. There were days when I could not walk, could not talk, and I mean that quite literally: I could not put one foot in front of the other. My mouth and tongue and larynx could not form words. I fantasized holding a gun to my head. I was constantly aware of the pharmaceutical drugs I had swiped from Steve's house, and what it would take to put me to sleep forever. I looked off the edges of buildings, calculating a straight drop down—no mania, all depression, all searching for the quickest way out.

Lauren's grief was manic. She wandered around Kīhei barefoot, smoking cigarette butts picked up from the ground, doing drugs with random people, surfing dangerous swells, ranting that tourists had destroyed Maui and she loved the island more than anyone. I wonder how many strangers saw her in that electrified state—that's how I picture her, blonde hair and blonde nerves all standing straight on end on some road in Kīhei—and thought she was a lost cause. Not worth saving.

Lauren let her grief loose on Facebook. She posted one hundred times in twenty-four hours, often in spare sentences, some disjointed paragraphs—once an entire essay—words screaming, pleading, bleeding on my computer screen. She wrote about peanuts on benches in Kīhei and awful anxiety and rust and sadness; Salinger and delicate edges and talking to the waves, her big feet thrashing in the sand; her bruised brain and her bruised body, booze and bad decisions, ugly snotty noses, limb-over-limb, who knew what? Marilyn Monroe and Carver and Ulysses, flashlights and rearview mirrors, the rains, the green, the lava, the shore, her island and him, Scottie Ass Robbins.

I'd never seen anyone grieve so hard. I'd never seen anyone grieve so publicly, either. My sorrow has been so internalized, so private, that many friends didn't know how far I'd fallen until I was already lifted back up again. Like some impressive sleight of hand where they missed the mysterious, but essential middle. I wrote to Lauren: *I know that when people tell you just hang in there, or just stay strong, they mean well. But I'm guessing you're tired of hanging in there, you're tired of being strong. I get that. I totally get that. So please, listen to me, know that I know what the hell I'm talking about when I say it can get better.*

I told her to go to an emergency room and tell them she's having a manic episode. If she's unable to say it, show them this text from me, I said. You're in a cycle that needs to be interrupted, I told her, and it *can* be interrupted.

I did not tell her: If the cycle is not interrupted, you are going to die.

* * *

I draw maps trying to connect the pieces of our lives, the fragments of their deaths. My mom died on January 4th, 1994 in Aurora, Colorado, and Scott died on January 3rd, 2012 in Aurora, exactly ten miles east of the house where my dad and Steve died. Scott died on January 3rd and my birthday is June 3rd. My dad was born on May 8th and died on June 8th and my brother was born on December 8th. The year Lauren was born is the same year I went to Maui for the first time. Maui, Denver, Aurora, the third, the fourth, the eighth, pills, pain, grief. I sketch Venn diagrams of dates and places, hoping the areas of overlap will create continents, and those continents will create a world. I print out Lauren's one hundred Facebook posts and cut them up into strips; I move them around and I paste them back together. I create poetry out of mania. I try to make something whole.

* * *

Not long before we were kicked off our surfboard table at Coconut's, I looked at Lauren and said, "I realize I only technically met you for the first time last week, but it seems like you're…well, okay. Are you? Okay?"

She seemed so grounded, so far from the woman picking up cigarette butts from the ground.

Lauren's blue eyes stared over her right shoulder, to the parking lot, like she was looking at herself in all those rear-view mirrors. "I am. I don't know what happened exactly, but I just got to a point where it was time to move on." From her grief and all the bad choices she made in its name.

Lauren and I hugged goodbye with the ocean behind us. It felt like the Maui I'd grown up on. There was, finally, some connection—and it wasn't about what was lost. Warm, young nights returned to my soul, the kind I could wade in forever. I pulled my car out of the parking lot and was stopped at a red light when the thin, cracked-out woman from earlier in the evening crossed in front of my car. She pointed at me and screamed. She pointed to the ocean and she pointed to the sky. I tried to look at her without seeming confrontational. "I see you," I wanted to say. That's the irony of being crazy; our behavior causes people to look away, to run. What we really want is to be seen.

* * *

This is the part where I tell you about a dream. This dream was archetypal and visceral, one I'd never had before and doubt I will ever have again.

The dream occurred before dawn on the day I left Maui. In it, I was standing on the lānai of my hotel room looking down on the ocean. Several blue porpoises played in the waves, diving in perfect arcs through the barrels, over the crests, under the water. Sunlight refracted off the water, but it wasn't blinding. I spotted the dark outline of a whale at the floor of the ocean. It was a giant, block-headed sperm whale, the kind Captain Ahab was obsessed with chasing across the sea. But I am no Ahab, no Ishmael, no Pequod. I am a woman living in fear of being consumed by grief.

With swift majesty, the behemoth rose to the surface in a complete breach, nose to the sky, chest in the air, fluke grazing the surface of the waves. It splashed back down on the whole of its belly, sending a tsunami towards me. The force of the water threw me back and up in the air, and I flailed. I danced in the wave. The only thing that ever seemed at risk, for even a moment, was dropping my cell phone into the sea. It slipped, but I managed to grab it, to hold on. I stayed connected. I stayed alive.

I thought I'd come to Maui to remember my past, to rediscover the threads of memory that had frayed with time. Crashing into the past was the only way to heal from it, I believed. But I'd remembered and recognized almost nothing. On my last day, I finally understood there was nothing more to recall or grasp onto. My life in Maui with my dad and Steve was ephemeral. Some people want to believe that we are more than a blip, that we leave a lasting impression on the places we've been. But my brother and dad and I were just tourists in Maui. We came and spent money and we left. It's all we were supposed to do.

The whale and the porpoises in my dream didn't speak, but I knew what they were saying: it's time. In the light of a Maui dawn, with saltwater sticking to my skin, I was no longer bound by the fear that I would be crushed by grief.

We will always see you, Lizzie, Lauren wrote in her Facebook frenzy two years earlier. *You are always going to go on walking. You are going to cross so many goddamn streets, we will have to wave in the rearview mirror.*

Epilogue

The Words, the Definitions, the Translation, and the Story in ʻŌlelo Hawaiʻi

hoʻomanaʻo	remember
ola	alive
makuahine	mother
makua kāne	father
kaikunāne	brother
kaikuahine	younger sister
kākou	we
maka mua	first time
kinohi	beginning, origin, genesis
olakino	health
ʻōpio	youth, youngster
waiwai	rich
mokulele	airplane
mokupuni	island
mea mākaʻikaʻi	visitor
kaʻahele	travel, a tour
hōkele	hotel
moana	ocean
kahakai	beach
pua	flower
nalu	wave
ua	rain
loulu	fan palm tree
hala kahiki	pineapple

mīkana	papaya
melia	plumeria
mōkuhikuhi	sweet
mauka	toward the mountain
makai	toward the sea
koholā	humpback whale
hauʻoli	happy
nani	pretty
makani	wind
moku	ship
moʻolelo	history, tradition
kaua	war
lanakila	conquer
aupuni mōʻī	kingdom
mōʻī	king
mōʻī wahine	queen
pilikia	trouble
ponoʻī	private
kūkulu	build
kanu	to plant
kō	sugarcane
mahi	plantation
kuleana	own
hana	work
kuapaʻa	slave, bonded servant
makani pāhili	hurricane
ʻiniki	piercing wind
pohō	out of luck, loss, damage
make loa	to die
aku	away from me

muli	last, after, behind
mea ola	survivor
'aha'ilono	the sole survivor carrying a message
iwi	bones
'uhane	spirit, ghost
pō	night, darkness, the realm of gods
kaumaha	heavy, weight, grief
makena	mourning, wailing
makemake	to miss, desire
lani	heaven
lōlō	crazy, feeble-minded
pupule	crazy
maha	rest, repose, freedom from pain
moe	sleep
pilikua	husband
mālama	care for, preserve, protect
maluhia	safety
ikaika	strong
ho'omaka hou	begin again
ho'oponopono	to make amends, make things right
kupuna	ancestor
pua	descendant
lehu	ashes
lana	floating
laulima	work together, cooperation
hoaloha	friend
hou	new again
nīnau	ask a question, inquire
nānā	observe
mana'o	thought, belief

akua	god
ao	clouds; also: light, daylight; also: world, earth
moeʻuhane	dream
kahiko	ancient
naiʻa	porpoise
palaoa	sperm whale
kai piʻi	rising tide, tsunami
huli	to turn, to curl over (as a wave)
lohe	hear, mind, listen, obey
kala	to loosen, unburden, absolve, forgive
kalana	forgiveness, release
mai poina	don't forget
hoʻomaikaʻi	grateful, gratitude
pūʻali	warrior
pau	end

Appendix A

The Aloha Spirit Law from Chapter 5 of the Hawai'i Revised Statutes

§ 5-7.5 "Aloha Spirit".

a) "**Aloha** Spirit" is the coordination of mind and heart within each person. It brings each person to the self. Each person must think and emote good feelings to others. In the contemplation and presence of the life force, "ALOHA," the following unuhi laulā loa may be used:

"**Akahai**," meaning kindness to be expressed with tenderness;

"**Lōkahi**," meaning unity, to be expressed with harmony;

"'**Olu'olu**," meaning agreeable, to be expressed with pleasantness;

"**Ha'aha'a**," meaning humility, to be expressed with modesty;

"**Ahonui**," meaning patience, to be expressed with perseverance.

These are traits of character that express the charm, warmth and sincerity of Hawaii's people. It was the working philosophy of native Hawaiians and was presented as a gift to the people of Hawai'i. "**Aloha**" is more than a word of greeting or farewell or a salutation. "**Aloha**" means mutual regard and affection and extends warmth in caring with no obligation in return. "**Aloha**" is the essence of relationships in which each person is important to every other person for collective existence. "**Aloha**" means to hear what is not said, to see what cannot be seen and to know the unknowable.

b) In exercising their power on behalf of the people and in fulfillment of their responsibilities, obligations, and service to the people, the legislature, governor, lieutenant governor, executive officers of each department, the chief justice, associate justices, and judges of the appellate, circuit, and district courts may contemplate and reside with the life force and give consideration to the "**Aloha Spirit**." [L 1986, c 202, § 1]

Appendix B

Miles's Banana Java Recipe

The last time I saw Miles the Bartender was on my honeymoon in 1994. He whipped up a batch of his famous Banana Javas for me and my husband, and I asked for his recipe. He spouted it off quickly as I scribbled it on a napkin. Years ago, I transferred it into my small binder of recipes cobbled together from friends and family over the years. The thing is, I've never actually made it.

When I returned to Maui in 2017, I saw the Banana Java on the menu of the poolside bar. Even though I'd been craving that exact drink for decades, I didn't order it. Miles wasn't there, and all my attempts at tracking him down had led to dead ends. Suddenly the drink became a metaphor for what was lost and could never be found. But for anyone else—for a normal person, let's say—it's just delicious. Enjoy it as you and imagine the topical stars and trade winds of Hawai'i.

In a blender, combine:
- 1 BANANA
- 1½ OZ KAHLÚA
- MILK OR HALF & HALF (AMOUNT NOT SPECIFIED, SO JUST WING IT)
- A SPLASH OF CRÈME DE BANANA

(although not included in the original recipe, adding some crushed ice would make it nice and slushy)

Enjoy!

Appendix C

WORKS CONSULTED

Books

Adler, Peter S. *Beyond Paradise: Encounters in Hawai'i Where the Tour Bus Never Runs*

Allen, Jennifer. *Malana Honua: Hokule'a—A Voyage of Hope*

Bird, Isabella L. *The Hawaiian Archipelago*

Collins, Lance D., and Isaka, Bianca. *Tourism Impacts West Maui*

Doughty, Andrew and Friedman, Harriett. *The Ultimate Kauai Guidebook: Kauai Revealed*

Engle Merry, Sally. *Colonizing Hawai'i: The Cultural Power of Law*

Farrell, Bryan H. *Hawaii, The Legend that Sells*

Grandy, Christopher. *Hawai'i Becalmed: Economic Lessons on the 1990s*

Haas, Michael. *Multicultural Hawaii: the Fabric of a Multiethnic Society*

Hemmings, Kaui Hart. *The Descendants*

Hibbard, Don. *Designing Paradise: The Allure of the Hawaiian Resort*

Mak, James. *Developing a Dream Destination: Tourism and Tourism Policy Planning in Hawai'i*

Mak, James. *Tourism and the Economy*

Māmaka Kaiao: A Modern Hawaiian Vocabulary: a compilation of Hawaiian words that have been created, collected, and approved by the Hawaiian Lexicon Committee from 1987 through 2000

McDermott, John, and Andrade, Naleen Naupaka. *People and Cultures of Hawai'i: The Evolution of Cultures and Ethnicity*

Schultz, Albert J. *The Voices of Eden: A History of Hawaiian Language Studies*

Shwartz, Sherwood and Lloyd. *Brady, Brady, Brady: The Complete Story of The Brady Bunch as Told by the Father/Son Team who Really Know*

US Department of the Interior. *Native Hawaiians Study Commission: Report on the Culture, Needs and Concerns of Native Hawaiians*, 1983

Vowell, Sarah. *Unfamiliar Fishes*

Williams, Barry. *Growing Up Brady: I Was a Teenage Greg*

Essays & Articles

Cooke, Dan. "Kauai burger joint fed hundreds in Iniki aftermath," *Hawaii News Now*, September 11, 2012

Drent, Les. "The History of Surfing," *Coffee Times*, Winter 2015-16

Didion, Joan. "In the Islands," *The White Album*

Didion, Joan. "Letter from Paradise, 21° 19' N., 157° 52' W," Joan Didion, *Slouching Towards Bethlehem*

Didion, Joan. "Where Tonight Show Guests Go to Rest," *Esquire*, October 1976

Essoyan, Susan. "1 Year After Hurricane Iniki, Kauai Puts Up a Good Front," *Los Angeles Times*, September 11, 1993

Gehrien, Rachel. "Community rallies to save mon-keypod trees in Koloa," *The Garden Island News*, December 14, 2007

Giacobee, Alyssa. "The Aloha Project,"

Hale, Constance. "The Hula Movement," *The Atlantic*, July/August 2002

Hitt, Christine. "Keepers of the Flame: How cultural practitioners are preserving Niihau's unique traditions," *Hawai'i Magazine*, May 2016

Kerr, Keoki. "Lanai resort will reopen in February with 75% increase in lowest rates," *Hawaii News Now*, November 20, 2015

Kutner, Max. "Surfers, Sunsets, and Dancing Girls: How Air Travel Came to Hawaii," *Smithsonian.com*, July 25, 2014

Jackson, Kristin, "A look at Hawaii's truly remote islands, Niihau and Kaho'olawe," *Seattle Times*, March 29, 2015

Lyte, Brittany. "Hawaiian Natives have been waiting since 1920 for promised land," *Al Jazeera America*, July 11, 2015

Lyte, Brittany. "Leaving Lanai: A billionaire's Hawaii could displace longtime residents," *Al Jazeera America*, February 14, 2016

Mooallem, Jon. "Larry Ellison Bought an Island in Hawaii. Now What?" *The New York Times Magazine*, September 23, 2014

Nagourney, Adam. "Tiny Hawaiian Island Will See if New Owner Tilts at Windmills," *The New York Times*, August 22, 2012

Petranik, Steve. "Editor's Note: We Work with Words, But Some Challenge Us," *Hawaii Business*, January 2015

Reynolds, Christopher. "With lots of Hawaiian beach resorts competing for your business, Maui's southwestern coast offers several luxury choices. So, in these tough economic times…Why Wailea?" *Los Angeles Times*, July 11, 1993

Roig, Suzanne. "Outrigger Canoe Club hits 100 years, *Honolulu Advertiser*, May 4, 2008

Roth, Randall. "Deconstructing The Descendants: How George Clooney Ennobled Old Hawaiian Trusts and Made the Rule Against Perpetuities Sexy," http://www.randallroth.com/files/

ESSAY%20on%20The%20Descendants%20as%20 of%209-4-2013.pdf

Shifrin, Carole. "Machinists Strike United Airlines," *The Washington Post*, March 31, 1979

Tsai, Michael. "Hawaiian Renaissance," *The Honolulu Advertiser*, August 16, 2009

Turner, Wallace. "600 Living on a Private Hawaiian Island," *The New York Times*, December 23, 1982

Websites

2015 Annual Visitor Research Report, Hawai'i Tourism Authority, http://www.hawaiitourismauthority.org

Archibald v. Cinerama Hawaiian Hotels, Inc., https:// law.justia.com/cases/california/court-of-appeal/3d/73/152.html

Big Five, HawaiiHistory.org, http://www.hawaiihistory.org

Get the Facts: Information About Energy Efficiency, Hawai'i Energy, https://dev424.hawaiienergy. com/about/get-the-facts

Hawai'i's Workforce: A Look at Characteristics by Industry, State of Hawai'i, Department of Business, Economics Development and Tourism,

Research and Analytics Division, December 2010, http://files.hawaii.gov/dbedt/census/acs/Report/2010-workforce-by-industry.pdf

The History of Hula, Ka ʻImi Naʻauao o Hawaiʻi Nei Institute, http://www.kaimi.org/education/history-of-hula/

Kapolei Mall Project Moves Forward, http://dhhl.hawaii.gov/2014/12/01/kapolei-mall-moves-forward/

Native Hawaiians in Hawaiʻi's Tourism Sector, State of Hawaiʻi, Department of Business, Economics Development and Tourism, Research and Analytics Division, April 2017, http://files.hawaii.gov/dbedt/economic/reports/Native_Hawaiians_in_Tourism_Final_4-13-17.pdf

Nā Puka Weheehe ʻŌlelo Hawaiʻi, http://wehewehe.org

Film & TV

30 for 30, "Hawaiian: the Legend of Eddie Aikau," directed by Sam George, ESPN Films, 2013

The Brady Bunch, "Hawaii Bound," "Pass the Tabu," "The Tiki Caves," directed by Jack Arnold, written by Sherwood Schwartz, Paramount Television, 1972

The Descendants, directed by Alexander Payne, written by Alexander Payne, Nat Faxon, & Jim Rash, Fox Searchlight Pictures, 2011

Hurricane 'Iniki: The Piercing Wind Before During and After, Island Television

Talk Story Bookstore: The Western-Most Bookstore in the United States, A Kauai Documentary, by Lance Matsumoto, https://www.youtube.com/watch?v=OcXcxKHlOmk

Previous Publications

The following essays were previously published in:

"To 'Okina or Not to 'Okina" and "A Haole Guide to Hawaiian Taxonomy," *Baltimore Review*

"Flying Under Assumed Names," *Origins Journal*

"Bombs Away," *Hawai'i Pacific Review*

"Descendant(s)," *Potomac Review*

"Return to The Kahala," *Carolina Quarterly*

Mahalo Nui Loa

A BOOK LIVES INSIDE A WRITER'S HEAD AND COMPUTER for years, and it's daunting to finally release it into the world. ENDLESS THANKS to Pat McDonald and Rachel Bell for seeing and believing in my vision for this project, and for giving it a safe place to land. Mahalo nui loa to the Hawaiʻi Public Library system for providing amazing source material along with fragrant trade winds. To Joan Didion for her writings about and around the fragrant trade winds. Mahalo to the people who told me their stories: Edie Jones (who taught me the meaning of hānai), Jim Jones, Robyn Russell, Nancy Kramer, and Duane Whitehurst. Mahalo nui loa to Karen Karbo for her invaluable feedback and coffee dates, and Aaron Gilbreath for not pulling any punches; To my Denver luau crew: Susan and Victor Chayet, and Andrea Tenenbaum; To the friends who keep me afloat in the rising tides: Michelle DeShong, Jackie Shannon Hollis, Yuvi Zalkow, Laura Stanfill, Scott Sparling, Jen Miller, Sarah Einstein, Lidia Yuknavitch, and Ron MacLean; To the travel companions who shared my love of the Islands and put up with my Cliff Clavin-like constant recitation of Hawaiʻi trivia: Michelle (again), Jackie (again, I'm sensing a pattern, here), Jennifer Graham, and Gaynl Keefe; To the eighties posse who were a big part of my coming of age, of my falling in love: Andy Rex, Donna Brady, Miles Figueira, Bobby Henry, and my big brother Steve; Mahalo nui loa to my beloved, Michael Keefe—my ahi, my wai, my ʻāina, my ea; And to Pete, for giving me the privilege of falling in love with Hawaiʻi.

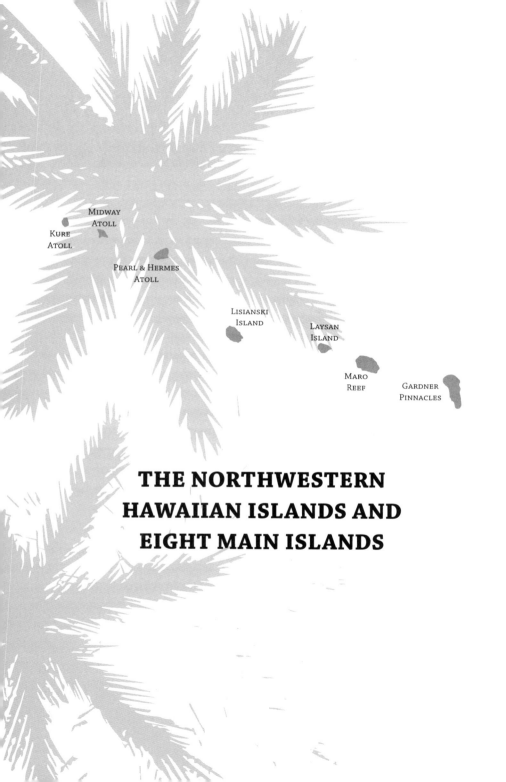

KURE
ATOLL

MIDWAY
ATOLL

PEARL & HERMES
ATOLL

LISIANSKI
ISLAND

LAYSAN
ISLAND

MARO
REEF

GARDNER
PINNACLES

THE NORTHWESTERN
HAWAIIAN ISLANDS AND
EIGHT MAIN ISLANDS

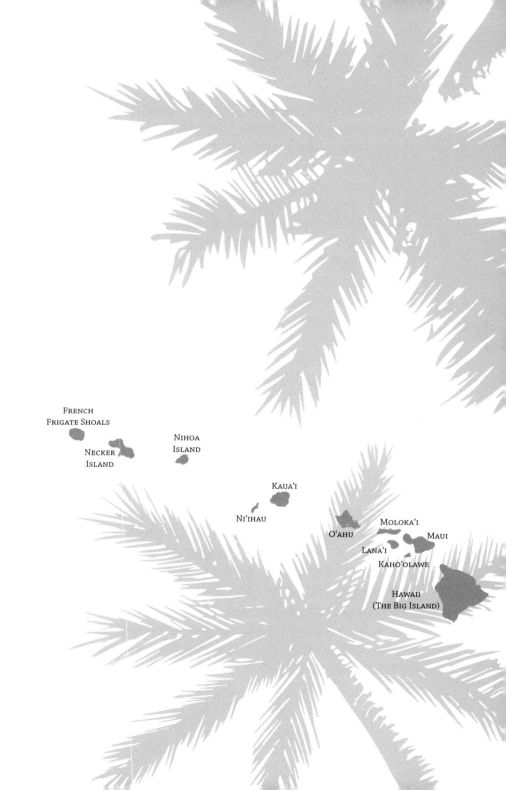

FRENCH
FRIGATE SHOALS

NECKER
ISLAND

NIHOA
ISLAND

KAUA'I

NI'IHAU

O'AHU

MOLOKA'I

MAUI

LANA'I

KAHO'OLAWE

HAWAII
(THE BIG ISLAND)

About the Author

LIZ PRATO IS THE AUTHOR OF THE SHORT STORY COLLECTION *Baby's on Fire: Stories* (Press 53, 2015). Her work has appeared in over two-dozen literary journals including *The Rumpus*, *Baltimore Review*, and *Salon*. She is editor at large for Forest Avenue Press. Liz teaches in Portland and at literary festivals across the country. She lives in a house in the woods with her husband, an indie bookseller and writer.